The Christmas Note

By Trenton Hughes

The Christmas Note

A novel by Trenton Hughes

Copyright © 2012 by Trenton Hughes

Cover Design by Shanique Flynn

Printed in the United States of America

First Printing: November 2012

First Kindle Edition: November 2012

ISBN 978-1480194755

Memories are the basis of our lives. Experiences are the basis of memories. An experience does not need to be personal; it simply needs to be experienced. This journey is a story of Christmas. This is not a traditional Christmas story that most are used to. This is an experience that would never be forgotten, and thus becomes a memory. Hopefully this can help to inspire lives, but most importantly, Christmas spirit.

Chapter 1

Claire and Ayden drove down the rain-filled streets. The Thanksgiving dinner and night at Claire's parents left their spirits high and stomachs full. They had about an hour's drive ahead of them as they neared the freeway headed back home to Campbell, Washington.

Claire looked up at Ayden with a grin. She adored the way he looked in knit sweaters that seemed to only come out during the holidays. The gray sweater he had on was the one she had got him last year as a present. He preferred the nice computer she had given him, but he still loved the little things like the sweater. He wasn't going to say anything as he knew how much she loved picking them out, picturing how he would look in them. Usually Ayden didn't even attempt to pick out clothes for Claire as everything he had ever tried to get her to wear was kindly exchanged for something more her style.

Ayden looked over to her and smiled as rain hit against the windshield in a subtle pattern. He continued down the freeway as he took his right hand and grabbed hers. Their hands rested against the center console of the Silver Volvo S60. With her free hand, Claire adjusted the heat to warm the car against the cold night and rain just outside. Then she moved her hand up to turn on the local Christmas music station. "O Holy Night" came on and both Claire and Ayden stared forward, hand in hand, truly happy.

Claire and Ayden had been married for just over three years now and were just as in love as ever, if not more so. They'd met when some mutual friends introduced them about five years prior. Both had been new to town as each was starting a new job. Campbell is a town of about fifty-thousand people. Even though it houses a few major businesses, people are still drawn to it for its strong sense of community. Ayden had moved from California to pursue financial advising with a good firm in Campbell. He'd moved from Irvine, where he'd been born and raised and had graduated with a Masters in Finance from UC Irvine. His parents had both passed away from heart attacks a year apart from each other by the time he was twenty. Nevertheless, over the years he had tried to move on and develop his life while trying not to dwell on that fact. He was twenty-nine now and was able to live comfortably from a job that he actually enjoyed.

Claire was from the town that her parents still lived in, Kentsboro, Washington. She had gone to the University of Washington in Seattle and finished with a Bachelor's degree in advertising. She moved back to Kentsboro a couple of years after working for an advertising agency in Seattle. After not being able to find work in her field, she moved to Campbell for a good job at an agency there. It wasn't too far from her hometown and she loved Campbell's ambiance. Everyone was neighborly and the town was gorgeous. It was known as the greenest city in the state of Washington. People were also drawn to it for its beautiful central park near a downtown that truly felt like the town's center. Now she was twenty-seven, and she absolutely loved everything about her life.

Each had moved to Campbell within a few months of each other. There was a group of about fifteen friends that hung out regularly; some married, some dating, some single. Both Claire and Ayden had a friend from the group that worked with them at their offices. Claire had hung out with the group about five times by the time Ayden was introduced. Claire always had a lot of fun with them and regularly hung out with some, including her new best friend, Myla.

It was December 11th, and Ayden had moved to town only a couple of weeks earlier. His new friend at work, Ben, had invited him to a town event that came around every holiday season, Christmas in the Park. At the beautiful central park, Campbell put on a Christmas event where the entire park was decorated with lights. In the center of the park was a giant Christmas tree that stood over forty feet tall. Santa would sit under it at night for children to tell him their Christmas wishes. There was also a walkway that led through the array of decorations and trees. One of the best perks was free hot chocolate to accompany the chilly winter nights. There was even a choir that sang Christmas songs around a live nativity scene. People would come from miles around to go to Christmas in the Park and everyone loved the joy it brought to the season.

Ben was going to meet up with his group of friends that evening for the event, and Ayden, not knowing anyone or the town, decided it could be fun to go along. Ayden's eyes lit up as he saw the hundreds of people in the park surrounded by thousands of endless twinkling lights. The huge tree in the middle was spectacular. It was decorated with ornaments all the way to its top. Children were lined up to sit on Santa's lap and a choir was singing. To Ayden, the scene was like something out of a movie. He smiled as they got out and headed into the park. A teenager handed them each a cup of cocoa. The night's air was crisp and cool so each had worn jeans and a couple of layers. Ayden wore a red and green sweater, trying to stay warm.

"They're right over there man, follow me," Ben said as they walked through the crowd sipping their rich, hot cocoa.

Ayden looked over to see a group of twenty something's mingling amongst themselves. There were six guys and eight girls.

"Hey guys," Ben called to them as they approached. Several of them shouted back their own greetings. "This is Ayden. I work with him and he just moved to town."

They focused their attention on Ayden. People introduced themselves to him one by one. After a few introductions, he noticed her.

His gaze lingered as she looked right back at him, smiling. He was mesmerized by the average-height brunette woman smiling with welcoming light brown eyes and bangs stretched across her forehead. She wore a touch of makeup but her thin face was naturally beautiful. She wore jeans with a nice black pea coat and red scarf. She was absolutely gorgeous. Finally he looked away and back to the others as he made his rounds and continued to introduce himself.

After a few more, she was next in line. Of course there were other attractive women in the group, but none caught his attention like she did.

"Hi," she said, catching him off guard. She smiled a shy smile, looking up at him as their eyes met. He couldn't help but grin.

"Hi, I'm Ayden," he replied, trying to regain his composure. He held out his hand for her to grab. She did, with a soft hand that when it touched him, he swore sent an electric wave rushing through his body.

"I caught that from Ben. I'm Claire," she answered back, still smiling.

"Nice to meet you Claire," Ayden responded. She captivated him and he didn't quite know why.

The night went on and Ayden got to know the entire group. They talked and he truly enjoyed himself as they walked, observing all the lights and decorations. There was a true Christmas spirit in the air and he loved it. He loved hearing the choir sing Christmas songs in the background and watching children excited to see Santa. He was getting to know his new friends and they all made an effort to make him feel included. For some reason, he couldn't stop glancing over at Claire. She seemed to talk mostly to one of the other girls, Myla. Of course Ayden had checked her ring finger and found nothing, to his delight. He didn't normally approach women, so even though she captivated him, he felt he probably would never do anything about it.

A few minutes passed and Ayden found himself at the back of the group walking alone. He wasn't lonely or sad; in fact he was content and happy. He was just looking around enjoying the Christmas spirit that he hadn't felt in years. He'd glanced forward to look at Claire quickly when she looked back at the same instant and caught him looking. Sheepishly he looked away, trying to play it off as a mistake. She stopped for a second to wait for him.

"Hey," Claire said to him as she stood at his side, now walking with him behind the group just in front of them.

"Hey. So how are you liking Christmas in the Park?" he asked, trying to strike up conversation. He felt a little nervous talking to her and he didn't know why, as usually he was a pretty confident guy.

"I love it. How about you?" she asked, smiling in an almost teasing tone.

"I do too. So how long have you lived in Campbell?" Ayden asked curiously, wanting to know more about her.

"Just a little over a month. Moved here for work. I heard Ben say you were new, but where did you move from?" Claire asked as they strolled side by side.

Before he could answer, the entire group turned around to look at them. He froze, surprised by all the attention.

Everyone smiled and a few giggled.

"Look above you," one of the girls said as Ayden stood next to Claire.

Each looked up simultaneously. The group started talking and laughing. "Kiss!" someone called.

Hanging above them was mistletoe. Ayden didn't know that mistletoe was a real thing and certainly didn't know what to do. His thoughts raced a million miles a second. Everyone stared as his nerves took over. He looked down at Claire who was looking right up at him. She smiled with that shy, cute smile and he couldn't help but admire her.

"Kiss! Kiss! Kiss!" the group of friends started chanting. Ayden didn't know what to do. She was smiling but would she want to kiss him? He had just met her for goodness sake! He knew he wanted to, but his nerves were in full force.

Suddenly she stepped in. They stared into each other's eyes. All at once he leaned in as she did the same and their eyes closed. Their lips met and it was like magic. All of his nerves melted away at the touch of her lips. He felt alive as they kissed. It was like nothing else mattered and it was just him and her. The feeling was incredible and he never wanted it to end.

Slowly they pulled away from the kiss and each looked at each other. She grinned as if she'd just done the most incredible thing she'd ever done in her entire life. He couldn't help but grin as well.

The group cheered and chanted as it ended. "Whew!" someone called.

Slowly they turned back around and started walking again. Ayden didn't know what to do now. His mind and nerves raced. Instinctively, he took a step forward to follow the group, then she did as well; each still smiling.

After a few moments, he felt something. She'd slipped her hand into his and they continued on through the Christmas in the Park. The glistening lights and beautiful Christmas carols blurred into the background.

Five years had passed since then and they were still truly in love. The car continued forward through the rain, and Claire and Ayden were hand in hand, peaceful with carols still playing on the radio.

"So, babe," Claire said as Ayden glanced over at her quickly. "What time should we start Black Friday shopping? Two? Three?"

Ayden grinned. "I was thinking maybe I would skip it this year. We're going to be so tired by the time we get home," he replied as his eyes stayed on the wet, dark freeway.

"No, no, no! We have done it every year since we've been married and it's a tradition! Plus, we will be home in like half an hour so that's bologney," she answered sharply giving him an "I'm in charge" sort of look.

He laughed. "It was worth a try. Well let's at least get a couple hours of sleep then go. How about three?" he replied playfully, squeezing her hand.

"Ha, you are too funny," she replied sarcastically. "Three it is," she continued. He smiled as "Chestnuts Roasting on an Open Fire" came onto the radio. Claire leaned over and kissed him on the cheek.

Chapter 2

Beep Beep Beep Beep. Came an annoying noise in the dark, weary hour of two a.m. Slowly Claire and Ayden woke up after only a couple hours of sleep. Nonetheless, it was a tradition and once they were out, they always enjoyed it. Ayden groaned as Claire leaned in and kissed him. Groggily he kissed her back. They got up and ready in what seemed to be dozens of layers of clothing as the weather in the beginning of winter in Washington at three in the morning was anything but above freezing.

***

The Volvo pulled into Campbell's outdoor shopping center. Normally the shopping center was busy, but never like this. Who would have thought that three in the morning would be the busiest the shopping center would ever be? The car maneuvered down aisles as finally they found a spot at the end.

People were lined up outside Target for what felt like miles. Everyone had on warm clothes protecting themselves against the weather that was sure to provide frostbite to anyone not fully clothed. Although it was early, dark and cold, everyone was excited and ready to go into the warm store to see what deals it held. The Christmas season was officially kicking off.

Claire and Ayden loved the feeling Black Friday provided to start off the season with a bang. They'd made it a tradition to make every Christmas season magical. They stood in the line, each smiling while thinking they would never get to enter the store with the size of the line ahead of them.

Claire snuggled up to Ayden trying to stay warm. He wrapped his arms around her lovingly. Soon after, the line started going. People became excited as they finally began to move and their Christmas shopping endeavors could begin.

Once they entered the store, Claire leaned in to Ayden and kissed him softly. "You know the rules," Claire said to him in the chaos of the store. "No spying on each other and we will meet back at the front in one hour." She scooted off through the madness of people and he began to do the same.

Ayden was suddenly struck by a sharp pain in his back. He bent over for a moment to regain his composure as the sensation felt like needles poking into his spine. He had felt this pain a couple other times recently, but each time he didn't think much of it. He shrugged it off as though it was no big deal, stood up, and continued through the store.

The deals must have been incredible with the amount of people in the store rushing around like it was the end of the world. Traditionally, Claire and Ayden each shopped for each other on Black Friday. She also shopped for her parents, and they each would shop for some of their mutual friends. Their list of people wasn't long as they didn't have children yet, or brothers and sisters, or nieces and nephews. They had talked about children and wanted them. They planned to wait five years after getting married till they were completely financially stable enough to do so. They had talked about it a lot lately as they already were stable, but they still had two years to go. Each felt that the day would most likely come sooner rather than at that five-year mark. Nonetheless, it hadn't happened yet.

Claire found a bunch of items for prices that would have easily been double normally. She was sure he would love some of the electronics she found.

Ayden always had a tough time finding the right gifts for her. He knew she liked clothes, jewelry, perfume, music, and active wear, but other than that she was tough. They always went to Target, then followed that by Macy's. Macy's would be where he would find most of her items but for now he scanned the deals to find some workout gear, a sweater, and music. He also found a few deals on things for his friends.

Each continued shopping for an hour and met at the entrance of the store at the deadline. They hid their bags from each other, grinning. They might try to peek in the next few days but each had managed to find hiding spots over the years that the other couldn't seem to find.

"How'd you do, babe?" Ayden asked grinning playfully while he stared at the six bags she tried to hide.

"No looking! And fine, how about you?" she replied matter-of-factly.

"Good, actually, there were some deals I was lucky to get as I almost got into a fist fight, bidding war, mugging, and a name calling match. Some people really get into the spirit, huh?" he finished sarcastically. People continued to swarm the store in massive amounts around them.

"Let's go to Macy's! They open at five," Claire announced excitedly as they walked out into the dark, cold winter's air once again.

They arrived at Macy's a half hour later to find themselves in another enormous line. It really felt like the Christmas season with the huge amount of people waiting in lines to shop for gifts for their loved ones. The feeling present was the reason Claire and Ayden had made it a tradition. They also didn't mind the great deals they managed to find on Black Friday.

Again Claire snuggled into Ayden as they waited in the anxious crowd of hundreds. They held each other to keep warm, neither wanting to let go.

Eventually the line moved again. Everyone entered the mall and Macy's in their scarves, beanies and mittens. As they entered, the warm air felt decadent in comparison to the bitingly cold air just outside. They held hands as they walked into the store.

Again Claire stopped and kissed him softly. She smiled, "see you in an hour sweetie," she said playfully and skipped off into the store. He laughed at her cuteness and walked into another store of chaos. People were everywhere. Ayden always felt a bit awkward shopping in the women's section, but on Black Friday it didn't seem to matter as everyone was just fighting for the deals.

Each searched for gifts, but this time just for each other. Claire would probably find a new sweater or jacket, a nice shirt, possibly shoes if she could find some he liked and a nice cologne or watch. Usually Ayden preferred the watch.

Like always, it was hard to please Claire with her taste in fashion. If he could he would buy some sort of outerwear like a jacket or sweater. He would also pick out the perfume he preferred best, as a win-win for both of them. Then he would always find some sort of jewelry. He began his hunt alongside the hundreds of others.

The Christmas music hummed in the background, barely noticeable over the noise of the enormous crowd in the store. Claire and Ayden met again at the front with their bags, each hiding from the other. "I see you found a thing or two?" she said smiling her cute, weary smile. He could tell that she was as sleep-deprived as he was.

He playfully grabbed at her bag, but she shuffled away. "I was just reaching for your hand honey," he said grinning. She gave him a sarcastic growl then each strolled out of the store, hand in hand.

Chapter 3

Claire and Ayden slept past noon as each had been completely drained after Black Friday shopping. It was Friday now and the weather had cleared from the night before. It was still cold, but there was no rain or snow yet. Claire came downstairs to the smell of something cooking.

When she saw it, she smiled. Ayden had prepared breakfast, well, a lunch breakfast, all for her. On the table sat a plate of eggs, sausage, toast and orange juice. It looked and smelled delicious. Normally each grabbed a quick bagel or protein bar on their way to work, but being a day off for the day after Thanksgiving, Ayden had time to make breakfast.

"Baby, you shouldn't have," Claire exclaimed and went in to kiss him on the cheek. He read the newspaper as he finished his plate of food. She sat next to him and grabbed the paper out of his hands. "Thanks," she continued jokingly.

"You're welcome. It sure felt nice to sleep in after the Black Friday madness," he replied looking at her begin her breakfast hungrily. "The weather is going to be nice today. I was thinking we could put up lights?"

She looked up excitedly from her breakfast. "That sounds like fun. And remember tonight the group is all going to practice for the Christmas Choir at church," she answered happily.

Their group of friends certainly did not all practice the same religion, nor did everyone love to sing or even have good voices. They just sang together to have fun with each other and enjoy the season. "Oh yeah, I forgot about that. Sounds good, babe. I'm going to shower then let's put up lights," Ayden replied as he got up from the table. He kissed Claire on the top of her brunette hair. She smiled and continued her breakfast as he made his way upstairs.

***

Claire came out to the garage wearing a red sweater and jeans that Ayden loved to see her in, as they showed off her figure. Ayden sat on the driveway preparing the boxes upon boxes of lights. Claire admired his figure too, as he wore a tight-fitted shirt and jeans that fit him nicely in her opinion.

"Looking good, hon," she called as she approached him. He winked back at her.

"Same to you," he said admiringly. "Ready?"

"Almost!" She ran back into the garage to turn on Christmas music. Every year they also made a tradition of listening to Christmas music as they put up lights. She'd be the one to put up the lights that she could reach around trees and the first story of their house. They had a modern-styled two-story townhouse so Ayden always did the second story windows and roof.

They began to hang the lights and chat while Christmas music played in the background. They always had fun just doing these simple Christmas chores. They lived in a community where all the houses were part of a subdivision in which all the homes looked similar. Most houses on the street had some sort of decorations. Some residents went absolutely all out. Claire and Ayden's house was very decorated and nice when it was done, but some houses were ones that the entire town would drive by to see. Because those houses were on their same street, the pressure was on for the rest of the neighbors, including Claire and Ayden. Claire and Ayden's house had icicle lights across the roof, colored lights around the windows, and a mix around bushes and trees. They had many lawn ornaments as well, like fake trees, snowmen and reindeer. Both continued to decorate, taking their time together.

***

Claire and Ayden drove down the road in their silver Ford Explorer. They headed to the church to meet their friends for Christmas Choir practice. Every year since they had moved to Campbell, they and all their friends sang in the Christmas Choir at the local church. A couple of the friends were members of the church, but most were not. It was just a great way for them all to have a good time together.

They drove the car into the church parking lot. They quickly recognized many of their friends' cars. After parking, Ayden quickly rounded the back to open the door for Claire.

"What a gentlemen," Claire replied and grabbed his hand. They entered the church to find about fifty people up in the stands, waiting to start rehearsal. They saw some of their friends in the corner waving to them. Each waved back. Eight were there already which meant that eight were still on their way. Over the last couple years the group lost some and gained others. Everyone looked ready for Christmas; hence being in the Christmas Choir.

"Hey guys!" Myla called over to them from the corner. She looked really happy and cozy in her red scarf, gray sweater and jeans.

"Hey, Myla!" each called back. Claire took the seat next to her friend and Ayden sat next to Claire. A moment later, Ben jogged in. He too looked cheerful in his winter-wear.

"Hey everyone!" he called, smiling. He shook hands with the guys and hugged all the girls before sitting next to Ayden. "Hey, man."

"Hey, haven't seen you in a few days. How you doing?" Ayden said.

"I know, I know. Good, really good. Went down to the family's place for Thanksgiving. How was your Thanksgiving?" Ben asked.

"It was really good. We went to Claire's parents and then did the Black Friday thing. So where is Shannon?" Ayden responded noticing he was alone.

"Yeah. Uh things didn't work out with her. It's okay, I am single and ready to mingle. Again," he replied grimly.

"I'm sorry, man. You know I'm still not sure why you and Myla haven't got together yet," Ayden said quietly as she was sitting just two seats away.

Ben got a bit nervous. "Shush man! I don't know about that. But we are here to sing, not worry about that." Ben looked over at Myla who was obviously beautiful. They had flirted a lot over the years but never done anything else. She was a mix of African American and French with stunning wavy hair and piercing eyes. He was a well-trimmed man, with a bit longer hair than most and a scruffy face that looked good on him. Most women found him attractive. For some reason, they had never yet moved past flirting though.

Moments later the conductor of the choir came to the stage. He said his greetings and went over what they'd be signing. After exchanging pleasantries, they began to practice.

They would practice every Friday till the Eve of Christmas. They sang a list of songs that they each knew well; some with better voices than others. They went through "Silent Night," "Christmas Cannon," "I Heard the Bells," "O Come All Ye Faithful," "Drummer Boy," "A Mighty Wave," and finished with "O Holy Night." The holiday spirit was almost tangible as they joyfully sang together.

Chapter 4

It was one of the best parts of his work day—lunch. It wasn't as though he didn't enjoy his job, because he did, but an occasional break was always great. His work gave him about an hour but they weren't actually counting. If he needed longer he was always allowed it. It was Monday after Thanksgiving weekend, and Ayden had errands to run on his lunch break. Unfortunately for him, one of those errands was a check-up at the doctor's. He had a few blood tests to take care of as the last month or so he had felt some unwanted pains. His doctor thought it best to at least check it out with tests, but told him there shouldn't be a need to worry.

He sat in the waiting area for about ten minutes past his appointment time. It was a given that the doctor's office never ran according to schedule. He waited around until they called him.

He made his way back, following the nurse. After a few routine measurements, he sat in another room waiting for about ten more minutes. Finally, the doctor came in. They discussed the tests he would be given. As expected, the doctor reassured him the tests were routine and shouldn't be anything to worry about.

They took the tests, and within an hour it was over and he was back in the car and headed to work. Of course Claire knew about the tests, but Ayden assured her the pains were probably normal and the doctor felt it shouldn't be a cause of worry. Claire listened to the words and didn't react. As he drove, he turned on the radio to hear the weather report. It predicted snow later in the night as well as the next day.

Campbell was not used to snow, so when it came, the citizen's panicked. They got snow maybe three times a year, and when it happened, roads, schools and businesses closed as a precaution. Of course, Ayden wouldn't mind a day of snow to add to their winter. It also wouldn't hurt to have a day off work. He continued driving back towards work for the second half of his day.

A few hours later he was back home waiting for Claire to get home from work. He decided to pick up Chinese takeout for dinner as both probably wouldn't want to cook after a long day back from Thanksgiving weekend.

Claire arrived looking stunning as always. He found her attractive when she wore her work dresses. She wore a black coat over her dress, accompanied by heels. She smiled as she entered and observed Ayden and dinner waiting for her.

"Hey baby," she called as she walked toward him. She leaned in and kissed him. She admired how cute he looked with his work clothes on. They kissed with the same romantic spark they always shared. They released and smiled, looking into each other's eyes.

They ate their dinners while discussing their days as they did on most nights after work. The storm was coming in and each hoped it would arrive in full force so that the town could go into its panic mode and they could have the day off work.

Once they finished with dinner, they went outside to plug in the lights and see how they looked. They had put in hours upon hours of work and it was time to see it pay off.

Ayden plugged them in as Claire stood patiently out in front waiting in the cold air that felt as though the snow storm could arrive at any moment.

Finally, the lights sparked on and the sight was breathtaking. Claire's eyes lit up as she looked at the icicle lights around the roof and colored bulbs around the windows. Even her work with the lights on the lower story, with lawn ornaments and trees looked good. Sure, others on the street looked equally as good if not much better, but it always felt great to be one providing some Christmas spirit as well.

Ayden rounded the corner and also looked up, mesmerized by the lights. He walked over to Claire and put his arm around her as each watched their house in awe. He leaned in and they kissed, feeling the romance in the cold night's air.

***

Ayden and Claire woke to the routine alarm clock that they so greatly hated to hear. Each groggily got up out of bed. Slowly, Ayden made his way to the bathroom as Claire stretched. She lifted the curtain to look outside without thinking.

Suddenly, she realized what had happened. She was in disbelief. She rubbed her eyes and continued to stare.

"Babe," she called to Ayden with some urgency.

"Huh?" he said, obviously still tired.

"Come! Quick!" she replied still staring out.

Ayden came out of the bathroom and went to the window as well. He couldn't believe it. He took a double take. Finally, he began to grin as he looked to Claire who was grinning right back at him.

Outside they could see down to the front lawn, which happened to be covered in white. A light snow was falling as they looked out.

"No work!" Ayden exclaimed, and hugged her out of excitement.

"It's beautiful," she said back, hugging him just as excited.

Quickly they put on their jackets and boots and headed for the door. They knew there wouldn't be work today as Campbell almost completely shut down whenever snow came to town. It was only a couple times a year that snow would fall, so when it did, it was always a treat.

Claire was dressed in her jeans and red cozy coat and Ayden in his black coat and jeans. Glee was in the air as each ran out the front door and into their very own winter wonderland. Grins were in full swing as they ran into the snow-filled yard and flakes fell from above. Claire observed the beauty of each individual molecule of a flake. It looked just like a paper mache snow flake, only much smaller.

Suddenly, something hit her hard. As she was falling backwards she realized what it was. Ayden had tackled her. They laughed, lying in the cold, wet snow.

Ayden began flailing his arms and legs as he made a snow angel. Then Claire joined in and made her own right next to him. She gracefully moved her arms and legs to make the perfect snow angel. Ayden got up to observe his and ruined it by getting up, making them both laugh. He reached for her hands as he cautiously helped Claire up. She got up without ruining her angel. They each stared at it, taking in its magnificence.

She looked up at Ayden as the light snow fell atop their heads. Each felt like a child. She leaned in and kissed him.

She pushed him away and grabbed a ball of snow. Before he realized what she was doing, his chest was pelted. She reached for more, then so did he. She threw another while laughing uncontrollably. He didn't want to hurt her so he threw one back at her stomach.

"Hey!" she said as if he wasn't supposed to throw one back. She reached for another and threw it. It splattered all over his face. It was cold and wet and hurt a little, but not enough for him to get mad. Suddenly, she froze not knowing if she had hurt him or not. He burst into laughter. Knowing he was okay, she did too.

"Let's make a snowman," he said.

"Let's do it!" she exclaimed. Each gathered around a thick plot of snow on the lawn. There was no need to worry about it melting since snow was still falling.

They continued to build the snowman in layers of balls from big to small. They playfully threw snow at each other and pushed each other over as they did. They truly enjoyed each other's company.

About an hour later, the snowman was done. Snowmen are much harder to make than they appear. This one looked a bit deformed, but nonetheless it was a snowman. The oval-shaped bottom was large and had a decent sized circular figure above it. Above that formed a head-like figure that had holes for eyes and a nose.

They stood back admiring their work. He put his arm around her as they watched the snow continue to fall over their snowman.

Chapter 5

The rest of the week passed smoothly. The holiday spirit was in full swing thanks to the snow that fell earlier in the week. It was Friday, December 4th and Christmas was rapidly approaching. The workweek was over for Claire and Ayden, and they were ready to enjoy each other.

"Hey, babe," Claire said as she entered the house smiling at Ayden sitting on the sofa.

"Hey, sweetie," he called back. She rounded the corner and went over to him from behind. He tilted his head back and she bent in for a kiss.

"How was work?" Ayden asked as he read the newspaper. She made her way over to the kitchen to grab a glass of egg nog.

"Pretty good," she said. "How about you?"

"Not bad. Not bad," he replied, still reading the paper. "So I was thinking tonight we could maybe stay in and watch a Christmas movie."

"Oh, babe. Remember?" she paused. "We are supposed to drive out to my parents' for the Kentsboro Holiday Festival," she answered to remind him.

"Oh I completely forgot about that! Why don't we just go next weekend? I am bushed from work and just want to stay in tonight. Plus it's raining and it's supposed to get pretty bad tonight," he said, putting his newspaper down.

"I already promised my parents though. It won't be that bad. We can rest and watch a movie tomorrow instead."

Ayden stayed quiet for a minute trying to decide how to respond.

"Babe, please can we just stay in? I really am tired, I'm sure they will understand," he replied with a bit of a lazy tone.

"I promised. We need to go. My parents are expecting us and so are their friends. I haven't seen their friends in a year. We can't break plans," she answered with a slight attitude.

"Here, I'll call them and explain. I'm sure they will understand."

She began to get frustrated as she'd had a long day too and had looked forward to this all week. "Let's just go. I'll drive. You don't even have to talk if you don't want. We can't break our promise."

"I didn't promise anything. Let's just reschedule. Dang," he snapped back, clearly frustrated. His anger was beginning to get the best of him.

"Excuse me?" she said, shocked that he'd had that tone with her. "No, we are not going to reschedule. Now snap out of it and let's go."

"Snap out of it?" he shot back. "No, I'm not going. I have had a long day and I didn't promise a thing. Your parents are grownups. They will understand," he said, showing a lot of attitude now.

She stared at him as the situation was escalating now. They rarely fought, but from time to time their arguments could get out of hand as each was never willing to compromise.

"Ayden. We are going and if you don't stop this smart attitude you have there will be problems between us," Claire returned sharply.

He looked up at her, clearly angry. "Forget that. I'm not going and that's final," he said defiantly as now he was just sticking to his argument as a way of proving a point.

"Seriously? You are going to act like that?" she said, almost hurt.

"Yeah. I'm not going. I told you that already. Are you so incompetent that you can't understand what I'm not going means?" he responded harshly.

A tear fell down her face as sadness and hurt filled her inside. "Well, I'm going. If you are going to be like that we will have problems later and I will drive there alone," she said, lightly sobbing and trying to hide it from him.

"Like I said, I'm not going. If you are, whatever," Ayden replied. The moment he said it he knew he was wrong. He wasn't going to just give in though. He didn't want to go and he certainly was not going to be controlled by his wife. She'd get over it and they'd get along. They each needed time to calm down over this fight that really wasn't about much of anything.

"You're a jerk. Don't expect me back tonight," Claire shouted and quickly rushed out the door.

Ayden didn't know how things had escalated so quickly but they certainly had. He was not going to compromise. He wanted to stick to his guns. He didn't have to be controlled if he didn't want to go. She would be back in a few minutes after each blew off some steam. They would get along and each would come to their senses like

26

they always did. Until then, he would watch basketball and try to unwind.

He continued to sit on the couch and watch the game as time went by. The rain had picked up; he could hear it loud outside. It was now fully dark out and almost an hour had passed. He knew he shouldn't have done what he did and if he could do it over he probably would have just gone to her parents'. Nonetheless he didn't want to lower himself and lose the argument. She would be back and they would work it out.

Another couple hours passed and there was still no word from her. He had already eaten dinner and the rain was pouring now. He was worried but knew she was probably okay. He thought she would have at least called though. Clearly he had pissed her off.

At eleven, he decided to go to bed. He was worried, so he decided to call her cell.

He dialed her number. The tone came on and after a minute of no response, her voicemail picked up. He hung up and figured she was just angry. He would have to make it up to her tomorrow. He was tired and he would sleep on it, feeling stupid now that he was going to bed without his wife by his side.

He fell asleep alone hoping Claire would forgive him when he woke. He slept peacefully on.

***

Ring Ring Ring. Ring Ring Ring. Ring Ring Ring. Startled, Ayden woke. He looked over to his alarm clock to see that it was just after one a.m. In a daze, he reached for his cell phone. Thinking it must be Claire, he answered. He noticed that the call was coming from a number he didn't recognize though.

"Hello?" Ayden said groggily.

27

"Hello, Mr. Johnson?" a monotone man's voice answered.

"Yes?" he replied, curious now, as the man sounded serious and obviously knew his name.

"There has been an accident," the man replied.

Chapter 6

Panic struck him head on with the words the man had just spoken. His eyes were opened wide as his heart pounded a million miles an hour.

Finally after what felt like an eternity but was really only seconds, he responded, "What do you mean there's been an accident?"

"I'm sorry, Mr. Johnson," the officer replied. Ayden's whole body tensed as his nerves were at a high. "Your wife was in a car accident a couple hours ago. She was rushed over to the hospital. I was the officer on scene. We just identified her, which is why we are just notifying you now."

Ayden shook uncontrollably with fear. There wasn't just one emotion inside him, rather a combination of every bad emotion he had ever experienced. His mind was spinning as he tried to comprehend what he was hearing. Suddenly adrenaline kicked in. "Where is she?" he demanded into the phone.

"She is at O'Conner Hunt Hospital," the officer replied and was abruptly cut off when Ayden hung up the phone. In a daze he scrambled for his wallet and keys and ran out to the car, then began to drive.

The hospital was about a half an hour away. Ayden began to drive at nearly a hundred miles an hour and felt that was even too slow. He didn't know what to think except to fear for the situation. He just drove, trying to keep enough composure so that he wouldn't crash.

The drive, which normally should have taken half an hour, only took him nineteen minutes. He parked across two spots as close to the entrance as possible, then sprinted for his life into the hospital. He was greeted by a receptionist at a desk.

"Where is my wife? Claire Johnson!" he demanded as he shook with intense anxiety.

She looked down at her computer and searched, immediately recognizing the urgency in his voice. She gave him directions over to where she would be. He ran as hard as he had ever run before, nearly knocking over a patient and her nurse.

Within a minute he found himself in the Emergency Room waiting area. People stared as he had sprinted in.

"Where is my wife? Claire Johnson!" he yelled again, yearning to see his wife and find out how she was.

The receptionist gave him a finger signaling him to wait a minute and she walked into the back. Adrenaline was in full force as he had to stop himself from knocking down a door to see her.

Within a few more seconds what appeared to be a doctor entered the room from the back. He wore a white lab coat and held a solemn face.

Ayden stared at him, ready to strangle him if he didn't help.

"Mr. Johnson. This is not easy for me to say," the doctor said then paused. "Your wife didn't make it."

Ayden felt everything around him move in slow motion as his mind couldn't fully comprehend what he was hearing. He stood there, bewildered. It was as though he was dizzy to the point of not being able to see or think. Slowly he regained enough composure to feel his adrenaline and anxiety again. Now his nerves, fear and panic set back in.

He pushed the doctor out of the way and rushed into the hallway of hospital rooms. He passed a few, but they clearly were not Claire's. A few more passed and to his disbelief, she was there. He couldn't believe what he saw.

She lay lifeless on a bed; eyes closed. She was just as beautiful as she always was. Her forehead was a bit bloody and she wore a blanket over her still body. She was so pretty. It didn't matter what condition she was in, Ayden thought she was the most gorgeous woman in the world.

He stared at her from outside the door, longing for her to open her eyes and run into his arms. He wanted to go back to before the fight and just hold her forever. Slowly he walked to her side as he began to tremble uncontrollably.

He felt as if his entire body was about to explode. He was still in shock as he approached his beautiful, lifeless wife. He stood over her, staring, hoping her eyes would just open.

He began to shake furiously as tears welled up and blinded him. A nurse and the doctor came into the room, but stood at the door, giving him the space he needed.

The tears ran down unchecked. He trembled as he fell to his knees. He bent over her as he reached for her hand.

"No! No! No!" he yelled as his tears streamed down while he shook. "Claire. Baby!" he screamed with longing to bring her back. He slowly comprehended that she was dead.

"Why? Why God? Please! No!" he shouted. The nurse and doctor just watched as he wept. The nurse began to cry as well. A tear fell from the doctor's eye as he left the room.

Chapter 7

Claire's parents rushed to the hospital as soon as they were notified. Ayden couldn't muster the strength to do it, but luckily he was able to tell the nurse who to call. Myla and Ben came within an hour of being called at two in the morning.

Ayden did not leave Claire's side the entire time. He lay next to her for hours in a state of hysteria. He held her as he wept and shook for hours on end. He didn't want to convince himself that she could be gone. His mind could simply not fully comprehend the reality.

He watched his beautiful wife as she lay lifeless next to him. It had only been hours ago that they had last spoke. Of course the nature of the conversation hadn't been pleasant. He replayed the incident in his head over and over again. Each time he tried to convince himself that it wasn't real. He longed to go back and change what he had done. Why couldn't he have just agreed and have gone with her? That way they would have been together. She wouldn't have been in an accident, or at least they would have crashed together.

At times, he thought about stealing pills to join his wife. He looked at the sheets as a possible noose for a way out. He wanted to be with her again and these were the quickest ways to do that. His strength was gone though. All he could do was lay next to her.

He wasn't particularly religious and she hadn't been either. He did believe there was a Heaven, but by the same mark he believed that there was also a Hell. When he thought about it he knew she had to be in Heaven. From church, he remembered that suicide was a ticket to Hell. He didn't want to be separated from her permanently by making a mistake like that. How then could he be with her? Would it count if he had someone else kill him? He tried to fathom a solution as after an hour, his sadness turned to anger. He hated himself, and God. Fury poured out of him as he tried to find revenge. What seemed like hours passed and finally her parents came and soon after their friends did too.

Everyone was in tears, shock, and disbelief. Each tried to comfort him, but each also wanted their own comfort. Her parents as well as Myla and Ben tried with no success to get him to talk. Ayden ignored them as never ending tears continued to fall as he grasped Claire's lifeless hand.

The nurses and doctors let them stay in peace. Ayden didn't know if anyone knew the real story. It was his own fault. They had fought and that was why she was dead. Maybe if they knew that, they would kill him. Could that be his way out?

At five in the morning as the night's darkness began to fade and a brightness began to rise, he finally spoke. Ben held Myla in his arms as each cried. Her mother was now on the other side of Claire, kneeling while she stared into her eyes. Her father stood at the foot of the door, also weeping. "It's my fault," Ayden whispered with the last of his strength.

Everyone looked up at him, trying to suppress their dazes of disbelief and tears.

"We got into a fight," he continued and burst back into tears.

To his surprise, he felt a hand on his shoulder. He looked back to see Claire's father standing over him. His look was one of understanding.

"It's okay son. It was not your fault. Don't ever think that," her father said. The words were not what Ayden had expected. He expected someone to be so angry that they might kill him. At his words, Ayden just sobbed.

"Ayden. She knew you didn't mean it," her mother slowly replied moments later through her tears.

This astonished him as he'd thought that she would never be able to forgive him.

Soon after, Myla came from behind him and hugged him in support. Seconds later, his other shoulder had a hand on it. He looked up to see Ben. They all wept together with Claire's lifeless body at their side as the winter's morn began.

***

An entire day had passed from that morning. Ayden hadn't slept even a second. The entire day was one of tears. Not much talking occurred beyond that morning. No one knew what to even say. Each tried to support the other while gathering the support they needed themselves. She was gone. She had been such a large part of each of their lives. The thought of her being gone was truly unreal.

Ayden realized now that she was dead. He still knew it was his own fault. He wanted to join her. His problem was that he didn't know how. He wished he could have been the one to die and she could have lived. He ultimately wished he could rewind time and cherish her forever, never disagreeing with his beautiful wife again. She had been his everything.

Chapter 8

Seconds felt like hours, hours felt like days. Time seemed to stand still for Ayden as he wept more tears in just the few hours than he had his entire life. When it was time for them to leave the hospital to have Claire's body taken away, the feeling was unreal. He felt as though he was fighting for his life just to see her again. In a state of uncertainty and paranoia, he was held back by the doctors and his friends as they took her.

Once she had left the room, he collapsed to the floor, weeping.

***

Ben finally made it back to their house in Ayden's car. Myla had driven them both to the hospital. She drove her car back as Ayden, in a state of shock, was not suited to drive. Naturally, Ben volunteered to drive him. Claire's family had disappeared hours before without saying anything, and everyone not being of their right minds, just ignored it and continued to cry.

Ayden stared at the ground as he approached his door. Ben followed behind silently as he knew it wasn't the time to talk. They both went inside and said nothing.

They sat for hours on the couch, staring at the wall. Ben did so out of pity and support for his friend.

Rain fell outside, setting the solemn mood of the day. She was gone, and sun wouldn't do the feeling justice.

***

Ring Ring Ring. Ring Ring Ring. The unexpected deafening sound broke the silence of the day. Startled by the sudden ringing, both Ayden and Ben's eyes jolted to the source.

Ayden's phone rang loud. He looked down and recognized the number as his doctor's. In his state, the last thing he wanted to do was talk, and much less think about anything that wasn't Claire.

Something inside him told him to answer it as the doctor could have news about Claire.

The phone rang a few more times as they each stared at it.

After what felt like an eternity, he answered.

"Hello?" Ayden whispered through his lack of energy and countless tears.

"Hello, Mr. Johnson. This is Doctor Phillips," came a raspy elderly voice.

"Yes?" It was all that Ayden could manage.

"Your results came in," the voice returned and paused. He didn't know what to think as his mind truly was not thinking normally. What could be worse than today? He thought of nothing. "Maybe it would be best if you came into the office."

"No," Ayden snapped. "Tell me now," he finished coldly.

"Okay Mr. Johnson. This may not be easy to cope with but I'm afraid my job is to deliver this type of news," the doctor said, then paused for a long moment. "Ayden, you have cancer," he finished softly.

Ayden's heart sped into overdrive as his anxiety was even higher than before. Cancer? How? He was so young. What did it mean? Would he die? Then another thought crossed his mind. It could be his ticket to see his wife. His mind spun.

All he could manage was a laugh. He began to crack up. Soon, his laughter became uncontrollable. Ben stared, wondering what on earth could possibly spark this fit of laughter.

"Mr. Johnson?" the doctor asked in response to the unexpected laughter.

Ayden laughed some more.

Not knowing how to reply, the doctor continued. "The cancer is fast and fully developed. Your spine is nearly covered completely. I'm afraid we are too late to do anything about it. I know sometimes the symptoms aren't obvious, but your pains are definitely symptoms," the doctor let out in a bit of ramble. It was difficult for Ayden to comprehend everything that he was being told. "Ayden. The cancer is terminal. Even if you decided to go through therapy, I'm afraid it may only add a few days onto your life."

Suddenly, Ayden gained enough stamina to reply. "What do you mean a few days?"

The doctor paused and breathed into the phone, obviously in self contemplation. "At the rate the cancer is spreading, you have no more than three weeks. I'm so sorry Ayden."

Ayden's mind spun as the bit of information given to him was nearly impossible to believe. He was going to die in three weeks? He calculated it in his head and realized that three weeks was Christmas day. He felt fine now. The pains he had felt were minor and he'd only checked them out as a precaution. How could he have cancer? Terminal cancer. His wife had literally just passed away, which was still unreal, and now he was going to join her? Hours before, he would have done anything to have her back alive. He also would have done anything to die and be with her again. Then he realized that by dying this way, he wouldn't be committing suicide. He would just die as a sign of God. Had it been planned this way? A million thoughts popped into his head as he tried to fathom everything.

"Thank you, doctor," Ayden finally replied then hung up.

Ben stared at him in disbelief. "Cancer?" Ben asked in shock.

"Cancer," Ayden replied. "The doctor says I have cancer of the spine that is fully developed. He said I don't have more than three weeks. Three weeks is Christmas Day."

Ben seemed to be trying to understand everything he was being told. Their sad day of not talking while coping with Claire's death had not prepared him for anything like this.

"Are you joking?" Ben replied, not knowing what else to say.

"Nope," Ayden answered then laughed some more.

Ben couldn't help but laugh as the laughter seemed to be contagious.

He regained his composure quickly then looked into Ayden's eyes.

"I am so sorry, man. I don't know what to say. I am going to stay here with you. I'm here for you."

"It's okay, man. I thought all day that this had to be a dream. When I finally came to the realization that Claire was gone, I wanted to die. I just want to be with her. I got my wish. Much sooner than I ever could have imagined. I am surprisingly okay with it," Ayden said. Ben looked down and Ayden relaxed into the couch, feeling a bit of relief in his long sorrowful day. Who would have thought that his own death would bring him relief? His wife was gone, and soon, he would be too. They each sat on the couch, staring.

Although the thought did bring an ounce of joy, his spirits were still low. He was the reason Claire was dead. He wanted to rewind time and spend the Christmas season with her, cherishing her forever. He loved her so much. He wanted to spend every minute of every day with her. She was his everything and only thing. He missed her dearly and his endless tears couldn't display how sad and hopeless he really felt. Claire, his true love, was dead.

Chapter 9

Ben left a few hours later and Ayden went straight to his bed. Although he hadn't slept more than two hours in almost two days, he still couldn't fall asleep. He lay in his bed with his eyes wide open, missing his wife immensely.

Seconds felt like minutes and minutes faded into hours as he lay sleepless. The only thing he could think about was his wife. His love was lost.

Suddenly, out of the corner of his eye, Ayden saw something. He looked up into the corner of the pitch black room. He knew something was there. He did a double take and realized he was right. It couldn't be though. It didn't make any sense, but the sight was unmistakable to Ayden.

"Dad?" Ayden asked with his eyes wide open wondering if his lack of sleep was causing his eyes to play tricks on him. His dad had passed away years ago so he knew it couldn't be real, but then how did it explain his father standing at the foot of his bed, staring at him. He wore his same old flannel he used to, accompanied by jeans. His slick hair and scruffy face brought back a comfortable familiarity that Ayden missed dearly.

"Hello, son," his father's aged, haggard voice replied. Ayden pulled off his covers and sat up, now fully awake, his heart thudding at the sudden shock.

"Is it really you?" Ayden asked nervously as his fears of the unknown started to take hold. Ayden was sure his mind was playing tricks on him. With all that had happened, the overwhelming sorrow had to have taken its toll. The lack of sleep for two whole days had to have added to his craziness. He couldn't be sane.

"Yes, son, it's me," his father replied kindly with a gentle smile.

Ayden shook his head. "But how? You died years ago," Ayden asked, confused and certain he was losing it.

"Yes son. I did die. I am here tonight to deliver a message to you. I know the grief you are dealing with."

Ayden's mind was spinning. Could it be real? "A message? How are you here Dad?"

"Claire has died and now you are going to die too. You have three weeks to live. I know at this point life feels unbearable to you. You need to realize that life is worth living," his father said.

"How do you know this, Dad? How are you here? How—" Ayden asked anxiously.

His father interrupted him immediately. "There are two roads you can take. You can do what you are doing and most likely planning on doing, which is to sulk and feel sorry for what you did and never forgive yourself. Or you can take the second road. The second is to realize that you only have three weeks left. In realizing this, you will see that these are your last days to do everything you can while you are here on Earth. You can leave an impact and live your life to the fullest of its potential in the last days. The choice is yours, my son."

"How can I not feel sad and as though my life is over? My wife died and it's all my fault. Now I am going to die too," Ayden replied, feeling as though his father didn't understand what he was really going through.

42

"I love you, son. Make your decision wisely," his father said softly. The next instant, he was gone. Ayden jumped up. He looked all over the room but it was empty. Ayden knew that his father had been there. He had seen and heard him. Even if he wasn't stable and hadn't slept in two days, he knew what he saw. His father had been in his room. He opened the door and looked down the stairwell.

"Dad?" he called in a panic. He longed to see him if only for another instant. What did his father mean? He had two choices? Of course there was no way of enjoying himself knowing his wife was dead and he was going to die. Why would he even say such a thing?

Ayden contemplated whether or not it could have been real. He also kept thinking about what his father had said. He could sulk or live his life. He thought about Claire and how he just wanted to hold her in his arms. He thought of death and how he would soon be approaching it. The thought scared him. His mind wandered rapidly as he lay in his bed; alone.

Chapter 10

Two days passed since the night Ayden had seen his father. He did sleep for small amounts of time. He thought about his father's advice endlessly. In the end, he knew there was no way to enjoy the rest of his life. He had less than three weeks and not one second passed where he didn't think about Claire. He grew to hate everything now that she was gone. Everything reminded him of her, and he wanted her back. He was still trying to come to reality with the fact she was gone. He cried endless tears and ate nothing. He couldn't bring himself to take care of funeral arrangements, so her family did so. He missed her badly and tried coming to terms with the fact that he would be joining her soon.

Ayden looked scruffy, with bags under his eyes and a reddened face. He wore a black suit as he walked through the cemetery. It was more difficult than he ever could have imagined. Every step he took, he nearly turned around and ran. He wanted to run forever until it all went away.

Many others also dressed in black walked solemnly through the cemetery to Claire's gravesite. Dozens were already gathered there. Many people gave their condolences to Ayden, but he couldn't deal with it. He stayed silent and tried to focus on his wife. He thought back to their perfect life together. The first time he saw her. The first time he kissed her. Their wedding day. Just days ago, when they'd been enjoying the Christmas season and their traditions.

He continued walking as he approached the gravesite. The air had a chill to it and the sky was gray. The winter air didn't have the same romantic holiday feel that it had just days prior.

Dozens more gathered around mournfully. Tears were shed all around by the sudden death of a very likable woman.

A preacher spoke, followed by Claire's mother and father. Ayden had been given the opportunity to speak but had bluntly refused. He was not ready to talk about it yet as the pain was sharper than any he had ever felt. He went into a daze while the speakers spoke.

His mind kept wandering back to the night when his father had spoken to him. He knew he'd seen his dad. His father's message was clear, yet so ludicrous. His dad simply couldn't comprehend what Ayden was going through. If he could then he would never expect Ayden to enjoy the last bit of his life. His wife was dead and he only had a couple weeks to live.

The only person who knew about the cancer was Ben. He made Ben promise that he wouldn't say anything. Ayden was going through a difficult enough time and didn't want to have to deal with more people. He wanted to be left alone with his thoughts and despair. Although Ben was reluctant, he finally agreed he wouldn't put Ayden through that.

Ayden stood, this time not crying. Mourners spoke as Ayden thought about what his dad had meant. He looked around at the endless rows of graves. Each grave was an actual person that had lived on the Earth. Ayden began to realize that everyone goes through the same cycle. His wife had simply followed the cycle. It didn't make it any easier, but his mind began to churn. He kept thinking back to what both his doctor and father had told him; he had less than three weeks to live. He could sulk or enjoy the rest of his life. He continued to ponder it while the funeral went on in front of him.

***

Claire's casket was lowered into the ground. Everyone wept and wailed at the scene. Her picture stood at the grave's side. Everyone stared at the woman they all had grown to love. Ayden watched as his wife would be forever buried.

People left slowly and tearfully. Ayden stayed for hours more, sitting by his wife's side. He stared at her picture, taking in the essence of her beauty. He thought back to the feeling he'd had when he first met her. That night at the Christmas in the Park had been magical. He thought back to how beautiful she was. He realized she was just as beautiful today as she always was. She had been his best friend and lover.

As darkness approached and the chilly air set in, Ayden finally rose. By now he was alone in the evening. The Christmas feeling was not the same as it had been just days before. The feeling was now dark and dreary.

He took one look at the picture of his wife and bent towards it. He kissed it. A tear fell down his cheek as he turned away and walked out of the cemetery in his black suit.

Chapter 11

Ayden drove slowly down the streets of Campbell, headed home from the funeral. At times before the funeral, he felt as though he honestly wouldn't make it through. Luckily most people left him alone, and strangely enough, he didn't cry as much as he thought he would. The feeling, however, was still one of the hardest that he ever had to bear. It was nearly impossible watching his wife's lifeless body sent into the ground where it would rest forever.

The strangest part of the funeral for Ayden was his train of thought. He couldn't stop thinking about what his father had said to him. When looking around at the endless graves, he began to contemplate it even more. He could either sulk or live his life to the fullest.

Before his diagnoses, he had thought about what he would do if he knew he was going to die soon, as many people have from time to time. He, like many, had thought he would do the most amazing things he could if he knew he only had a small amount of time to live. Why now did he not feel the same when he knew exactly when he would die? He continued to drive down the street in contemplation.

He felt the urge to take the route by Christmas in the Park. It wasn't out of the way, but the urge felt odd. Ever since Claire had passed, he had grown to hate Christmas and everything about it. Christmas had been the time when they had met and fell in love. Christmas had been a magical tradition for them as their marriage grew. Christmas had been in full swing as they had done all their favorite holiday things just days ago. Christmas was the reason she was gone. She had driven back to a Christmas festival that Ayden should have gone with her to. Christmas was not the same to him anymore.

A few minutes later he saw it. The brilliant lights glistened in the winter night. The breathtaking trees were all decorated and festive. The park looked like it always did, adding a magical feel to the season. He drove by looking over, remembering how he had first met Claire. A tear fell as he continued on. He came to a red light alongside the park. His depression sunk in more as he now had no clue why he took the route. It just made him miss Claire incredibly more. He wanted her in the passenger seat, smiling by his side.

He waited at the red light and looked back over to the park. By now the park was emptying out as it was late and it had to be below freezing.

At that moment he saw something huddled on the ground. He looked back into the park near one of the lit Christmas trees. The huddled figure was unmistakably a person.

He looked closer to see what was clearly a homeless woman, probably in her thirties and very dirty looking, lying in a sleeping bag near a tree. He always pitied the homeless, but this felt different. The air was freezing and rain or even snow would most likely fall soon. How could she just sleep out in the park? He thought about how some people might find it offensive that she was lying in the middle of the Christmas in the Park. He knew that type of person all too well and he hated them.

As upsetting as the scene of the woman in a sleeping bag cuddled up next to a Christmas tree in the freezing winter's air was, there was nothing he could do.

The light turned green and Ayden faced forward and accelerated away. He was saddened by what he had seen, but that was just how it was.

He kept driving as his mind raced back to Claire, Christmas and his dad. He continued to let his mind wander in his depressed, dreary state.

He arrived at home and slowly walked in, reminiscing of walking in with Claire and watching her dazzling grin. He shut the garage as a feeling of loneliness sunk in. The day had been long, and every day felt as though it would never end.

Ayden walked past the kitchen and fell onto the couch. He sat back and loosened his tie as he stared blankly. He didn't bother to pick up the remote to the television or the stereo. He guessed that the rest of his life would most likely consist much of this same thing.

If Claire were alive, they would have been out with their friends or on a Christmas date. He wouldn't be sitting at home moping in agony missing her. His thoughts drifted back to his dad. Ayden knew he had seen him, and he kept thinking about how insane his advice of living his life to the fullest was. His pain was too much to do anything. Yet, he continued to ponder the words.

He sat on the couch staring for nearly half an hour. Suddenly, the thought of the homeless woman in Christmas in the Park popped into his head. He did feel bad that a woman, or anyone for that matter, would have no place to go and be forced to sleep in the freezing weather in an outdoor public place.

He turned his head around to look outside. As he suspected, rain had begun to fall. She was now outside, cuddled up next to a tree in the freezing night's rain. As lonely as he was, he felt she may be the one person on Earth lonelier.

Never before had he really helped a homeless person. He always wished there was something he could do, but honestly never knew what that was.

His father had told him he could mope, which did sound like the best option at the moment, or he could do all that he could with his life. In that moment he felt compelled. He popped off of the couch and got into his car.

He drove back towards Christmas in the Park in the rain of the winter's night. He tried to figure out what he would do once he saw her. Maybe he'd give her money or buy her food. He didn't know, but he felt this would be considered making a difference with his life. He thought of Claire and how this would have been something that she would have done. She probably would have stopped the car earlier to help the woman.

Moments later, he parked in front of Christmas in the Park. The lights were still lit on the endless Christmas trees. Decorations were everywhere, but people were not. It was nearly eight and the rain had most likely driven people home early. Ayden got out and walked toward the spot he had seen the woman.

He couldn't help but feel that he was being crazy as he walked towards her. It seemed like a good thing to do, but he was taking the advice of his dad, who could have easily been a figment of his imagination. He continued to walk as he wished he was doing it with Claire by his side.

Finally he saw her. Rain started beating harder as he bundled up in his jacket. The air was literally freezing as he felt the chill against his face. The woman lay in the same spot he had seen her earlier. The sight brought him even more sorrow. She was cuddled up in a sleeping bag on the sidewalk next to a lit Christmas tree. She had to be freezing. She appeared to be asleep, but shivering. She had nothing but her sleeping bag to shield the rain. She had a few dirty bags at her side, but not much else. He continued to walk toward her, not knowing how to approach.

She appeared to be maybe in her late thirties from the distance he was at. She had probably been homeless for quite some time judging by her dirty hair and face as well as her belongings. The sight was distressing.

He contemplated turning back since she was asleep. He thought maybe she didn't want to be bothered. Then he thought back again to his father's words. He could sulk or live the rest of his life the best he could. He knew what he needed to do.

"Excuse me, ma'am?" Ayden asked as he approached her side. The rain was falling hard now and he began to shiver.

The woman didn't move at all. He looked closer to make sure she was alive. He quickly realized she was still shivering.

He decided to try again. "Hello there," he said kindly.

Slowly, the woman opened her eyes and looked up at Ayden. She seemed startled and scared.

"Hi. Sorry I didn't mean to bother you. I just thought maybe I could take you to get a bite to eat inside somewhere. It's cold and rainy and," he trailed off, trying to make his case.

She stared at him, still seeming scared and unsure. She didn't reply as she continued shivering as rain hit her head.

"I promise I'm not a creep or anything. I just thought I'd ask if you would like to get something to eat inside someplace warm," he said trying to justify his actions.

She seemed hesitant, but sat up. "Uh," she paused. "Okay I guess," the woman said in a very soft, meager voice. Her voice didn't sound abnormal, just weary. He somewhat expected her to sound off in some way—crazy or perhaps intoxicated. Oddly enough, he realized this was the first time he had really talked to anyone without tearing up since Claire's death. He hadn't been able to bring himself to speak, but strangely, words came normally when trying to help the homeless woman.

Chapter 12

They arrived at the local Denny's a few minutes later. She trusted him enough for the time being to leave her bags in the car. She had also trusted him enough to get into his car. It took some hard convincing that he didn't have bad intentions. He did honestly just feel bad and he wanted to take his father's advice to try to make a difference while he was still on Earth. He knew buying a homeless woman a meal wouldn't do that, but it was at least a step in the right direction.

The rain fell hard as they entered the Denny's. A few people inside gave the duo odd looks, as he was well dressed and the older woman was obviously homeless. Ayden noticed the looks and hoped that she didn't.

So far, they hadn't spoke as she seemed not to want to and he wanted to respect her privacy. He still couldn't stop thinking about Claire and how he wished she was at his side. He missed her awfully and he tried constantly to hold back tears. He did his best as he sat across from the homeless woman whose name he didn't yet know. They ordered meals and ate in silence. Ayden didn't want to overstep a boundary so he decided to just let her eat. Each ate as though they hadn't eaten in days, which actually may have been true. Ayden hadn't even thought about eating for the last couple days. He began to wonder how long it had been since the woman across from him had eaten as well.

He wondered how often she was able to eat and the thought made him sad. He could eat any time he wanted, but across from him was a woman who probably rarely ate, and when she did eat, probably didn't eat much.

They ate for nearly half an hour. "How about dessert?" Ayden asked, breaking the silence from their delicious meals. He quickly thought of Claire and how she would always order a hot cocoa and apple pie. He wished he could watch her as she sipped her cocoa with her breathtaking smile.

The woman looked up. "Okay," she said mildly. "Can I get peach cobbler?"

"Of course. I'll have one too," he replied, then called over the waitress to order two peach cobblers and two milks.

"May I ask your name? I'm Ayden by the way," he said, trying to make small talk as he realized they hadn't even exchanged names.

"I'm Emma," she replied meagerly.

"Nice to meet you Emma," he said then stopped as he realized she didn't want small talk. The peach cobblers came and they ate the warm delicious desserts. He continued to think about Claire and his dad and how this might be his last peach cobbler as the days were ticking by.

Once they finished, they walked back to his car. "I don't mean to pry, but do you sleep at Christmas in the Park?" Ayden asked as they got into the car quickly trying to stay away from the hard rain and freezing air.

She seemed hesitant. "Sometimes."

He contemplated what to do for a minute. He was only going to live a couple weeks so why not give her some money to have at least a night indoors.

"Let me give you a little bit of money so you can get a hotel for a night. This rain is really falling," he said trying to make his point.

"No," she said flatly, which was not what he had expected. "Thank you for dinner sir. But that is quite enough. You can drop me off back at the park and I will be okay," she finished sternly.

He didn't know how to reply so he drove forward back toward the park.

"Here is my card in case you need anything. Seriously call any time," he said not knowing what else to do. He handed the card to her and she reluctantly took it. He felt bad. He wanted to make a difference as his father instructed, but it wasn't going how he'd expected. It had been difficult the entire time to hold back tears from the constant sorrow that he felt from Claire being gone.

He pulled up to the park and before he could get out to grab her bags, Emma had grabbed them already and opened the door. "Thank you, sir. You are a very kind man. God bless you," she said then left.

"You're welcome. Again feel free to call if you need anything at all. Goodbye," Ayden called out to her as she walked into the rain and colorfully lit Christmas in the Park.

As he drove off, he thought about God blessing him. So far that had been the exact opposite of what had happened. Claire was gone. If God was blessing him, Claire wouldn't be dead. They would be happy together celebrating the holiday season as they had been just days before. The rain beat against the windshield as he made his way back home; alone.

Chapter 13

He finally slept. The sleep had been short and terrifying. He woke over a hundred times looking around to where his wife normally lay. His night seemed more difficult than any before. Nightmares had crept in many times. He missed her badly. All night he thought about her, his dad and the homeless woman. His wife would have helped the woman and he knew that as a fact. He wished there was more he could have done to help. The woman had most likely slept in the freezing air and pouring rain. He honestly wanted to sulk for his last couple weeks, but the thought of making something of himself did sound admirable. The night had gone on full of sorrow and contemplation.

His day went on much the same without Ayden doing much of anything. He ate very little. As quickly as the day had come, it was passed just as fast.

Night came and he decided spontaneously to drive to Christmas in the Park. He didn't want to celebrate the season that he was growing to hate, but rather he wanted to see if the woman was out again in the cold. He knew that snow would be falling soon. He couldn't live with himself if he knew that the woman might be sleeping out in the snow.

Many times on the way over he looked at the passenger seat where his wife always sat by his side. He missed everything about her.

He looked up at the clouds in the rapidly darkening sky. It certainly looked like snow. Soon he approached Christmas in the Park.

Again the beautiful lights lit the trees and elegant Christmas in the Park. Most people had emptied out of the park. He looked over to the entrance where he had seen Emma the day before.

Sure enough, he saw something at the same spot he'd seen her the night before. His stomach churned as he felt a sadness for where the woman had to sleep. No one should have to live like that. He longed to help the woman as he felt every human should have a better life than that.

The woman appeared to be asleep again, cuddled up in her sleeping bag on the ground near the same Christmas tree.

Ayden pulled over, and then approached her as he had the previous night. "Hello, Emma," he called to her gently, trying not to wake her too harshly.

She looked up at him confused. "Hello," she replied sternly.

"I was driving by and was wondering if maybe you would like to grab a bite to eat again?" he said unsure of how to proceed.

She hesitated. "Are you stalking me?" she asked firmly.

Ayden had to laugh at her comment. "I promise I'm not. I honestly just want to help, nothing more." It was only the second time he had laughed since Claire had passed. He missed her tremendously but it still did feel nice.

She seemed reluctant. Then she got up. "Well, okay. Thank you, Ayden," she said as she gathered her bags. The air was cool and crisp and soon would be full of snow. Ayden grabbed her bags and put them in the car.

They drove back to Denny's.

Again, people gave them odd looks of uncertainty and scrutiny seeing a homeless woman with a decently dressed man. Ayden tried to let her be and allow her to talk only when she felt like it. He wished Claire was by his side so that they could both try to get to know the woman. Claire was definitely better at that type of thing. His thoughts drifted from his wife to his dad. Ayden didn't know if this was what he meant by making a difference, but he felt again like he was at least on the right track.

They each ate as if it were their first meals of the day, even though it was late. Time ticked by and neither spoke.

When they were finished with dinner, Ayden looked up at Emma. "Would you like dessert?"

She seemed shy at first, but then nodded her head.

"Great, what sounds good to you?" Ayden asked trying to be polite.

She paused a moment. "The peach cobbler was delicious with milk. Would that be alright?" she replied softly.

"Of course." He called over the waitress and ordered two peach cobblers and milks again.

They sat in silence for a while. Ayden was still too sad to focus much on trying to make conversation.

Suddenly she spoke. "You may be wondering why I am homeless. Don't worry, I would wonder too," she said.

He looked up, confused. "No, no. Don't worry that's not me at all."

"I'll tell you, it's okay," she responded, then paused. "Years ago I was married with a son. We lived here in Campbell," she continued then paused again. Ayden could tell this was difficult for her and may have been the first time she had told the story. He listened intently. "My son had just been born and everything was nice. My husband had a job and I was a stay at home mom. Shortly after my son was born, my husband left. We were renting our house so I had no place to go. He took every penny and left me and my son behind. I had no one I knew; no family or friends. I had no place to go. No one would hire me. My son is now six and he lives in an orphanage. I had to let him go. Not a day has passed where I haven't thought about him. I have struggled for six years to stay alive, but here I am," she finished then stared out the window.

The waitress brought the peach cobblers and milks. Ayden tried to take in the story. "I am so sorry," was all he could muster. He felt sadness for the woman. She had certainly had a rough life. He couldn't imagine what it would be like to have to give up a child. He couldn't imagine what it would be like to be homeless. He was just beginning to know the feeling of losing a love.

"It's okay. It's just my life," Emma replied while eating her cobbler.

"Since you told me your story, I will tell you mine," he said. Still choked up by her story, he took a bite of cobbler and paused. "I live here in Campbell. I lived here with my wife. A couple days ago we were supposed to go to her parent's place an hour away. We got into a fight because I didn't feel like going." He paused as a tear fell from his face. "She took off by herself into a harsh rainy night. She was hit head on and killed." He began to cry harder as he started to fall apart. It had been the first time he had talked to anyone about what happened. The pain inside was sharper than any he had felt before. He cried as he tried covering his face.

Suddenly something tapped him on the shoulder. He looked up to see the woman, dirty and at least ten years his senior standing there, crying as well. She held out her arms.

Ayden got up and hugged her. There was nothing romantic about the hug in any way. It was simply a sign of comfort. They each cried as other customers casually looked their way wondering what was going on. Ayden missed his wife badly. He needed her back.

***

After dinner, Ayden drove her back to Christmas in the Park. The lights were still lit and ornaments hung in the countless Christmas trees. The snow still hadn't started, but that would change at any moment.

"Emma, would you please let me give you a little money for a hotel? It will snow tonight and no one should need to sleep in that," he said. He may have pushed a boundary but he truly didn't feel anyone should sleep in snow.

"No," she replied flatly. They had grown a bit closer as each had shared their story with each other. "Thank you again for the meal though. You are a good man, Ayden," she said as she grabbed her bags. "I hope your sorrows lift. Your wife is a beautiful person and I can sense the love you each have for each other. I truly hope you will feel better. You need to know it was an accident," she finished then reached to shut the door. "Goodnight, and thank you again."

"Thank you, Emma." Her words struck him. It was so kind and also helpful to hear. Tears began to well up as he thought about the words and his wife. He wished Emma had taken money for a hotel. He didn't want her out in the cold another night. It wasn't his place to push her to do anything though. Sadness filled him as he drove back to his home to be by himself.

Chapter 14

The next day came and went quickly. Ayden hadn't had to go into work since his manager knew what had happened. He knew he couldn't muster the strength he needed to pull off a normal day of work anyways. The day passed much the same as the ones before—full of self-contemplation, tears, and sadness.

He didn't eat much yet again, as he didn't have the desire. Every bite of food reminded him of Claire and what she liked to eat. It was all too hard.

Night approached and the snow continued to fall. If Claire had been around they would have had a blast in the snow just like they had days ago. They would have been enjoying the Christmas season in all of its magic. She wasn't around though, she was in the ground and he would never get to see her again.

Time and time again he thought about religion and God. He had always believed, but this was a true test. He wanted to be with her again. All he could do was hope there was a heaven and if there was, that he would be worthy enough to make it there; to be reunited with Claire. He tried to keep his faith in God even though it was difficult knowing God had taken his wife. He still couldn't manage enough strength to pray. Strangely enough, as scary as it was, he was for the most part fine with the thought that he would die in a few short days. He continued the day full of thought and boredom.

Hours passed as the days dragged on. *Ring Ring Ring. Ring Ring Ring,* came a loud sudden burst of noise. Shocked, Ayden looked up and awoke from his daze. He looked around to find the phone. He hadn't heard from anyone lately, nor did he want to. He wondered who it could be. Maybe the doctor telling him the cancer was more rapid than anticipated?

He reached for the phone. "Hello?" he said softly through his weariness.

"Hey, man! It's Ben," his friend said with enthusiasm. "How are you today? I know it's been rough for all of us."

Although Ayden wanted to sulk some more and be left alone with his pain, it was somewhat nice to hear from his friend. "I'm okay. What's up?" Ayden replied trying to mask his sadness.

"Well, hey, I'm sure you probably want to be left alone, but I thought I would at least ask. We were going to go caroling and we were all hoping you would join us," Ben said sounding as though he knew Ayden wouldn't be interested.

Quickly his father's message came back to him. He could sulk or live his life while he still had it. "Okay, I'll go," he said, surprising himself.

Ben hadn't expected it. "Really? Okay, great man! I'll pick you up in an hour?" he replied excitedly.

"Sounds good," Ayden said, wondering what he'd got himself into.

"And, hey. I haven't said anything about the cancer to anyone. If you still don't want me to, I will respect your wishes. I just need you to know I am here for you." Ben waited for Ayden to reply.

"Thanks, Ben," Ayden said then hung up the phone. He knew Claire would have gone caroling. This was the type of thing they loved to do together during the Christmas season. It wouldn't be the same without her however. He tried to regain his composure enough to put on a face for the caroling.

Sorrow hit him as he missed Claire more and more. He ate a little trying to gather more strength, then showered and dressed warmly for caroling on a snowy winter's night.

Ben arrived in an hour and they drove off down the lit streets full of decorations. Ben was in slacks and a red sweater with his hair styled back nicely. Ayden wore a warm brown jacket and tan slacks as well, with his hair slicked to the side. It had been much nicer than anything he had done with it since Claire's passing.

"Everyone is going to meet us there. I'm really glad you came man," Ben said as he focused on the road ahead.

The only reason he had agreed to go out was because of his dad's words. "Thanks. So where exactly is 'there'?" he asked curious, still trying to hide his sadness. Normally Claire would have been in the car with them, leading the caroling.

"We are going to carol at the homeless shelter. Everyone should be there soon." Suddenly, Ayden thought of Emma. He still felt terrible that the woman had no house, and as a result was forced to sleep out in the cold in Christmas in the Park. The only meals she had eaten lately were probably from him. She had a tremendous strength that he would never know.

They arrived at the homeless shelter and were greeted by the rest of their friends. Each had been there at the funeral, but respectfully gave Ayden the space he needed the last few days. He could tell by their reactions that no one expected him to join them for caroling. He received hugs and small talk as each knew they shouldn't push him too far.

"I miss her so much Ayden," Myla said as they hugged. She wore a red and green sweater and jeans with her hair up.

Ayden tried to hold back tears at her comment. He thought of Claire and how happy they always were, hanging out with their friends. They released from the hug and Myla went over to Ben and grabbed his hand.

Ayden noticed the hand holding with surprise. He couldn't help but smile. He and Claire had tried to set them up numerous times as they had always flirted. Finally something must have happened.

They saw his smile and they each laughed. "Yes, we finally got together. Thanks to your and Claire's persistency," Myla said giddily.

He liked that Myla brought up Claire, whereas most tried not to bring her up. He didn't want to forget her.

"I'm glad," Ayden replied with a smile and the group of friends walked in together.

The shelter was like a giant cafeteria. Ayden knew there were rooms with beds and bathrooms somewhere else, but the room they were in was the dining area. Ayden was glad places like this existed as an option for the homeless as he thought about Emma sleeping out in the park. There were numerous tables filled with homeless people, dirty and unkempt. The sight was saddening, however, to see this amount of people homeless, waiting in a cafeteria-like room just to get some food. They all looked nervous and anxious. Many of them looked up at the group of people that had just walked in.

Ayden looked around the room in hopes that maybe Emma had decided to come to the shelter. He wished she would take advantage of the shelter and food. He looked around at all the people who looked sad and grimy. The sight was depressing. Each had bags and carts at their sides; their life belongings. He wished this type of life didn't have to exist.

Suddenly he saw her. Sure enough she sat at a table in the corner by herself. She looked up at him. She seemed a bit embarrassed at first, but gave a light smile. He realized that was the first time he had seen her smile. Even through the smile, she looked just as sad as before though.

The shelter's director introduced the group of friends to the homeless. They all looked up, curious as they waited for their dinners to be served.

Ayden tried not to think of how much he missed Claire, and tried to focus on Christmas, caroling, his friends, and the homeless. He knew this was what his dad meant by living his life.

They began to sing a few carols. They started with "Joy to the World" then went to "Silent Night." Then they sang the "Twelve days of Christmas." Myla yelled out to the crowd to join in for the last one.

They sang "Jingle Bells" by kicking it off with "Dashing Through the Snow." To Ayden's surprise, most of the homeless began to sing as well. The sound was harmonious and beautiful. The feeling in the room was breathtaking. His hairs began to stand with the goose bumps he felt. To his astonishment, everyone seemed to be singing. The song was beautiful and mood incredible, with smiles all around.

After the caroling, the friends dispersed throughout the room, some mingling with the homeless and some to serve the food. Ayden was glad he had come. As easy as it would have been to sulk and cry at home by himself, helping out felt nice.

He walked over to the corner. Emma sat there by herself staring up at him.

"I'm glad to see you here," he said, breaking the silence. She gestured for him to sit across from her. Someone brought them both a plate of food. Ayden didn't know whether or not to take it, but he didn't want to offend her, so he took the plate.

"Thanks. That was nice of you guys to sing," she said softly as she began to eat. Her hair was stringy and wet, obviously dampened by the snow. It saddened him that she slept in it.

"Yeah, my friends convinced me to go," he replied, taking a bite of his mashed potatoes.

"I can imagine it must be hard. With your wife passing just days ago. I don't know how I would handle it."

He realized she was becoming more comfortable with him.

"It is hard. I have just as much respect for you. You have truly been through a lot," he replied while scooping some peas onto his spoon.

They continued to eat in silence while his friends did their own things in the shelter. After they finished their meals, Ayden looked up.

"I don't want to overstep a boundary, but I want to meet your son. Have you ever thought about going to see him?" he asked not knowing if he had gone too far.

Emma stayed silent for a long while. "No. Thank you, but I can't," she replied sternly.

He had somewhat expected it, but it was saddening to hear. He felt deflated knowing he had crossed a line.

They finished eating then said goodbye and Ayden joined his friends.

His friends said their goodbyes and gave hugs. Everyone expressed how nice it was to see Ayden. He appreciated the support and love. He wished so badly that Claire could have done it all with him. That most likely would be his last time caroling.

Chapter 15

The next day came as his life seemed to be ticking away faster and faster. The day went much the same; full of contemplation, sitting, and sadness. It was only afternoon, and to his surprise the snow had faded and the sun had come out. It was still chilly, but there was sun.

The shrill sound of the phone awoke Ayden from his thoughts. He looked over wondering who it could be; probably his friends or doctor.

"Hello?"

"Hi," came a soft, tired voice. "This is Emma. I got your number from the card you gave me."

"Hey Emma. How are you doing?" Ayden asked, surprised to hear from her.

"Okay. I wanted to invite you to look at Christmas presents with me," she said. He was surprised by her request. He didn't think she Christmas shopped due to the fact she was homeless. Quickly he thought about what his wife would do and his father's words. He knew what he should do, but so badly he just wanted to sit and sulk.

"That would be great," Ayden said. They planned where and when to meet, then Ayden got ready. He wore his red sweater that Claire had picked out for him just a few Christmases ago. If only she could see that he'd put it on without a fuss.

***

Ayden and Emma arrived at the mall a short while later. Ayden thought back to just a few days ago when he and his wife had been at the mall to shop for Black Friday. He still had her gifts, and the gifts she had bought were sure to be somewhere in the house. The thought brought a tear to his eye, which he quickly tried to hide.

Emma still looked clearly homeless and received many odd looks inside the mall. Ayden didn't care how people felt. He wished they would be more respectful as she was a human being with every right to be at the mall.

"So, are you picking anything out today?" Ayden asked curiously.

They continued to stroll around as she looked into a store. "No," she said then paused. "Every Christmas I like to go to the mall and look. I imagine people's reactions if only I could give them the presents. The thought of it always makes me happy. So I go around the mall looking and picturing how people would react if they got the gifts," she replied softly as they walked.

He had expected her to be looking for herself rather than others. It was a terrible thought to think she simply wanted to give gifts but couldn't afford to. She was quite admirable.

"That is really nice. Most people would secretly look for themselves," he replied looking into stores. "Why don't you show me things you think people would like?" He decided to let her enjoy herself.

They went into a few clothing stores. "This is something my friend James would love," she said holding a large leather jacket. Ayden smiled and she continued to a hoodie. "And Fred always said he wanted a hoodie. And this beanie would be perfect for Jim," she said holding up a

70

beanie. He thought about it and wondered who these people she was talking about were.

They left the store and walked by a dress store. Ayden noticed Emma looking in intently as they passed. Ayden thought back a couple years to when he and Claire had gone on a date to dress shop in that very store. The thought made him simultaneously happy and sad.

They went into a candle store. "Pretty much everyone I know would love a candle. Some of them really smell bad. Smell this one, vanilla spice." She held a candle to his nose. The sweet smell of vanilla reminded him of baking cookies with Claire. He found it ironic that she found that others smelled bad when she herself did too, but he wouldn't say anything.

Next they made their way to a women's clothing store. "Isn't this sweater beautiful? Jenny would love this!" Emma said holding a pink sweater with fur that looked warm. She walked over to the jeans. "My friend Mona always said she wanted jeans." She held up a pair. Ayden smiled and nodded. He really didn't mind the shopping. He wished he had been more patient with his wife when shopping. If he could, he would trade a lifetime of shopping with Claire to have her back. "And this!" she said pointing to a heart necklace. "Harriet would love this. I think Harriet is my best friend," Emma finished simply.

"These are all beautiful. I'm glad you took me to do this," he said. He knew it would offend her to offer to buy the clothes, so he didn't bother. He wished that he could do more for the poor homeless woman.

"Thank you for taking me. I do love the Christmas season. People are more giving," she said. He knew she wasn't talking about them giving to herself. She genuinely liked that people were nicer around the Christmas season. Ayden was still growing to hate the season as it had been such a tradition for him and Claire. Nonetheless, he went along with it wishing it would all end sooner and that he would hopefully join her in heaven. He wanted her back, and until that happened, he would long to see her again. They continued around the mall looking at gifts and talking. They each loosened up more so than when they had first met. It felt to Ayden that Emma was almost like a long lost sister that had just had a rough life. They continued on through the Christmas-decorated mall filled with people of all sorts.

Chapter 16

It was Saturday December 13th. Ayden had two weeks left to live and just about two weeks till Christmas day. The Christmas season was passing, but full of sorrow. As much as he missed Claire, he continued to think about what his dad had said. He could sulk or live the rest of his life as best as he could.

He got into his silver Ford Explorer and drove down to the mall to do some shopping. It was nearly impossible to leave the house as sulking yet again sounded much better, but he left, knowing maybe he had a chance to make a difference.

He went to each store Emma had showed him. At the time he took mental notes of every item Emma mentioned. He found each one in each store. He bought them all and had them wrapped by the cashiers. He bought the clothes for the men she mentioned, ten candles for whomever, the clothes for the women and the necklace for her best friend. Ayden didn't know how she would react, but he hoped she would at least take the gifts to give out. She had been so happy just thinking about giving them out. She had a rough enough life, so he figured he would try to at least do this much. In the end, he spent nearly five hundred dollars on everything. As a financial advisor, he justified it by realizing that he was going to die in two weeks anyways. He had a lot of money saved up, and there really wasn't anyone to pass any of it on to.

After all the presents were bought and wrapped, he decided to head down to see if Emma was at Christmas in the Park. Even if Claire were still alive, Ayden knew she would support something like this. She might have been a little skeptical of the cost, but Claire was the type of person that was always giving. He wondered how Claire would have dealt with him dying if the roles were reversed. The thought saddened him. The pain he had felt losing her was something he wouldn't wish upon anyone, so he was glad that she would at least never experience it.

He arrived at Christmas in the Park, greeted by thousands upon thousands of bright lights carefully hung around endless rows of Christmas trees. As depressed as he was, he still realized the scene was amazing.

To his luck, he spotted her in the same spot. He wondered if she slept in the same spot every night. How could someone bear the cold, lonely nights outdoors like that?

He pulled over and approached her, carrying all the presents. This time she wasn't asleep. Immediately she looked up at him in shock.

Ayden tried to read her expression, but couldn't. "Hey," he called.

"What is that?" she asked in an annoyed tone.

He braced himself. "I don't want you to feel bad at all. I just thought of how nice it would be for you to give all of those people the gifts," he said, then placed the boxes by her side. He had remembered the names she had said, and thus placed name tags on each box.

Emma didn't seem to know how to react. "Take them back. I don't need your help! Why do you keep trying to help me like I am some charity case! I didn't ask for anything," she snapped.

He tried to gather his thoughts. "No! I would never think that. I just enjoy spending time with you. I mean, since my wife has passed, I have been miserable. You have helped me to open my eyes and have a new perspective on things. I only bought the gifts because I thought those people might enjoy them. I'm sorry," he said, trying to make his case as honestly as he could. He really didn't have bad intentions with the homeless woman. He simply was trying to take his father's advice as best as he could, even if his father hadn't really been there.

She hesitated. Then her expression softened. He guessed it was due to his bringing up Claire. He wished Claire were there. She was always better at dealing with the conflicts. "Okay then," was all Emma said.

"Great. I'll just leave them here and you can give them out yourself," he said looking at the gifts.

"Thank you, Ayden. You really are a good person," she said back looking down at all the gifts.

"No, thank you. You are the one helping me. Any chance I can give you money for a hotel?" he asked, pressing his luck.

"No," she said flatly. "Thank you, Ayden. You really shouldn't have. God bless you. Goodnight."

"Goodnight," Ayden replied, then walked back to his Ford Explorer through the Christmas trees and decorations.

Chapter 17

Ayden woke the next morning to the phone. "Hello?" he asked into the phone as he woke, depressed yet again.

"Hello, Mr. Johnson. This is Dr. Phillips. I was just checking in on you. How are you holding up? I can't imagine well."

Ayden tried to wake enough to answer the question. "Surprisingly, Doctor, that hasn't been my struggle. I mean it is scary thinking I will die in two weeks, but the hardest part is knowing my wife is dead. I have never been so down in all my life. It really is unbearable," he said to his astonishment. It had really been the first time that he expressed through words how he felt.

"I can't even imagine what you have had to deal with. How are the pains?" he asked.

Ayden thought about it. "Honestly Doc, I haven't felt them. I feel pretty healthy. I find that odd."

"Hm. That is odd. Maybe you could come down to do some more tests?" the doctor asked.

"Maybe. We'll see," Ayden replied.

"I'm glad the pain hasn't been bad yet. Ayden I do wish you the best. You are so strong. Call me if you need anything," Dr. Phillips replied.

Ayden noted the word *yet*. He hoped he wouldn't have any pain. It seemed unlikely seeing as he hadn't felt it yet. He also wondered how he would die without feeling pain though. "Thanks, Doctor," Ayden replied then hung up.

***

The day passed much the same as the others when Ayden was interrupted by yet another phone call. He answered. "Hello?"

"Hello, Ayden. It's Emma. I was wondering if maybe we could eat?" Ayden looked at the clock as he had debated about going to church all day. He decided he would have enough time either way. If he was going to make it into heaven, he felt going to church may be something he should do.

"That would be great," he answered. They planned where and when to meet, then Ayden dressed in slacks and a button down white shirt and tie in case he decided to go to church. He decided to take off the tie until then so that he wouldn't offend Emma by being overdressed. He held onto the tie that Claire had got for him last Christmas. He wished she could see him wear it. He wished they were going to church together.

***

Ayden and Emma arrived yet again at Denny's. Again came the same looks of scrutiny they'd drawn previously. It was clearly obvious there was nothing romantic, but they still drew whispers. Again Ayden hoped she didn't notice.

They ordered in silence. He hurt inside, longing to see Claire again, if only for an instant.

77

"Thank you for taking me," she said breaking the silence. He looked at her. She looked as though she hadn't showered in a year which made him feel bad.

"Thank you for asking," he replied and their meals were brought over. She began eating her pot pie as he bit into his chicken breast.

"I used to come here with my mom when I was a kid. I always loved it," she said, then smiled and took another bite.

"Tell me about her," he said curiously.

She thought for a moment and took another bite. "She was great. So loving. She was a single mom just caring for me. She worked and went to school. One day, she was walking across a street and was hit by a car. I was a teenager at the time. She didn't make it. From there, I went on my own until I met my ex-husband."

He thought about her story. She really had dealt with incredible struggles. "I am so sorry," he said, unsure of what else to say.

"It's okay. It all happens for a reason." Ayden took a bite wondering why such hardships had to exist. All he wanted was people to stay alive. Was that really so hard?

"I liked coming here with Claire too. She would always order the apple pie. I always pictured us coming here with a child. It is just a comfortable place," he said thinking of the past.

"That really sounds nice. I wish I could have met her. She sounds like an angel."

"She was. She was perfect," he said as tears began to form. He missed her dearly. A tear fell down Emma's face as well.

They finished their food and ordered cobblers and milk again. When they were done, Ayden thought back to his father's advice. "Would you like to go with me to church? I have been debating on it all day. It really is hard, but I think it might be good to go," he asked as his tears were now gone.

She contemplated it. Ayden wondered if she was a churchgoer. He doubted she went, looking the way she did. He assumed she may be too embarrassed. He did notice that she had said "God Bless" to him a few times however.

"Sure," she said shyly.

He hoped she would handle it okay as he drove the Explorer toward the church he and Claire attended once in a while with some of their friends. It was the church he and Claire had gone to just days prior to practice for the Christmas choir.

They walked into the church to find most of the rows were full. People looked up at them with a bit of suspicion. Ayden quickly noticed the looks and hoped they didn't make Emma uncomfortable. People should have no right to judge, especially in a church. Nonetheless, people looked and whispered as Ayden and Emma found seats in the corner.

They sat through the entire service, enjoying the speakers and singers. Many of the messages and songs shared related to Christmas and giving. Ayden appreciated the words, as hard as it was to sit in the church without Claire. He assumed people would wonder if he was okay just a week after her death. They would also wonder about the homeless woman he'd brought to church. He wished he could just be left alone to try to listen to the words of the speakers.

To his delight, Emma didn't seem bothered by the looks, and she also seemed to enjoy the church service. As much as he still hated Christmas as it was part of the reason Claire was dead, he appreciated the message. He could only hope that church was one step closer to seeing his wife again. He tried to hide his tears and pain as he wished his wife were by his side listening to the messages and hymns of Christmas.

Chapter 18

Monday approached and yet again, Ayden didn't go to work. His work knew his situation with his wife and didn't expect him back for a while. Without work, he didn't have much to do. Each day passed with nothing but thinking and sadness. Each day consisted of many tears and conflicting thoughts. He needed her back. He didn't care about his own health, he just cared about Claire.

Hours passed with the Christmas spirit definitely not in the air. He did, however, continue to think about his dad's message. He wondered if helping the homeless woman counted as what he'd meant. He hoped he was making a difference of some sort.

After more time passed and the cold night came, he decided to head out to the store. He spent hours upon hours in Macy's picking out items. He got a dress for church for Emma. The woman working helped him through it all. He figured she was a small as she was nearly all bone. Then he went over to find a comfortable pair of jeans. The woman helped him find a warm jacket and a shirt. Last, he went over to the shoes. They picked out a pair of walking shoes as well. He finished by grabbing socks and figured he would give her money if she wanted to get underwear. He hoped Emma wouldn't take offense to his gesture. He simply wanted her to have better clothes for winter. The woman rang everything up for again a total around five hundred dollars. If Claire were with him, she would have been able to pick out clothes in no time. Come to think of it, maybe not. Claire loved shopping and she was known to shop for hours.

He drove the Explorer yet again to Christmas in the Park. His eyes were met by the dazzling twinkling lights in the Christmas trees. He parked with his bag of clothing and walked to her normal spot.

Sure enough, she was there. It was a cold night yet again and Emma was cuddled up in her sleeping bag near the same tree.

She looked up as he approached. "Look. If you don't want these, that's okay, but I just wanted to at least try. I remember you got mad last time. I just want to assure you I don't think you are a charity case. I just felt an impulse to get these. And by now you know I still have the best intentions. I feel like you are a sister I never knew," he finished, trying to make his case before she became upset which he knew she would. He knew he probably would too, if the roles were reversed.

She looked into the bag curiously. She began to pull out each item. She looked at the shoes, socks, shirt, jeans and dress. He tried to read her reaction.

She looked up at him with tears in her eyes. "Thank you, Ayden," she said as she burst into tears.

He didn't know what to think. He had expected her to be upset. He felt relief and happiness as she seemed to accept the clothes. "If you want to buy underwear, I put a twenty in the jean's pocket," he said unsure of how to proceed.

She laughed through her tears. "You really are a good person. God bless you, Ayden."

He smiled back. He wished there was more he could do. He shivered in the cold night as he looked around at the Christmas decorations everywhere. "Thank you." If only Claire were with him to feel the joy of seeing the homeless woman enjoy new clothes.

Chapter 19

His life was ticking away before his eyes. Tuesday came and was leaving just as fast. He had less than two weeks to live. There were less than two weeks till Christmas as well. Yet again, most of his day consisted of sitting around staring at walls and thinking about Claire. He didn't understand how someone could move on from the death of their spouse. The thought seemed impossible.

He also thought about Emma and the troubles she had gone through. He couldn't imagine how painful it would be to have to give up her own child. He truly wished she had an easier life.

If Claire were alive, they would have been out with friends, singing carols, watching Christmas movies, looking at lights, getting hot cocoa, helping the homeless, practicing for choir, having a white elephant night and so much more. Their Christmas season would have been filled with fun times that would become great memories. None of that was going to happen now. She was gone. He thought about the presents he had bought and didn't know what to do with them. He thought about her presents she had bought. He wondered if he should try to find them, but decided against it as the pain would be too much. He couldn't bear to think about that now.

Time passed and again, Ayden was woken from his daze by the phone. He reached over to pick up the phone instinctively.

"Hello?" Ayden asked into the phone.

"Hello, Ayden. It's Emma," the voice replied softly.

"Hey, Emma, what's up?" Ayden asked. He wondered if she had to use the pay phone when she called him. He felt bad if that were the case.

"Well, I was wondering if you could come to the park to visit," she asked shyly.

Ayden accepted. He didn't do it out of obligation as he did indeed want to help and see her. She helped him too. His father's message helped him get up though. It helped him to realize that he was able to make a difference. He still didn't know how big that difference was, but he was sure it was more than if he sat around sulking all day. He tried to compose himself enough to go see Emma.

He arrived half an hour later in the usual spot; the entrance to Christmas in the Park. The lights were not yet illuminating the trees. Daylight hung in the air, sure to fade soon enough. The park was mostly empty, but as always, Emma was near the same Christmas tree. This time, she wasn't lying in her sleeping bag. She sat next to the tree bundled in the jacket Ayden had given her the night prior.

Ayden waved as Emma looked up. He was relieved to see she had on her new jacket and shoes. Immediately he noticed something in her hand.

She held a wrapped gift. It struck him as odd as he simply didn't expect her to be holding a gift, and wrapped at that. He could tell from the wrapping that it was not one of the ones he had purchased from the mall.

She looked up shyly. Even though she wore the nice new clothes, her hair and face gave her away as homeless. She looked dirty and tired.

"This is for you," she said as she remained seated and lifted the wrapped gift toward him.

"For me?" was all he could manage to say. He didn't expect anything from her; she was homeless for goodness sake. He began to feel guilty taking a gift from her.

He took the gift and looked down at her before he began to unwrap it. "You really shouldn't have," he said in a comforting voice.

He unwrapped the paper to find a red, hand-knitted blanket. The knitting was near perfect and looked as though it had to have taken weeks if not months. He knew immediately that she had made it. She had bought the materials and wrapping paper and knitted the blanket herself, which must have taken endless hours. Guilt and sympathy flooded in.

There were no words that could express the gratitude he felt. Tears formed as he held them in. He knew the state the woman was in, and it certainly was not one to give gifts. What a beautifully giving person she was.

Emma didn't seem to know how to respond. "I'm sorry, did I do something wrong? Does it remind you of Claire?" she asked in her shy, meager voice.

"No! No," he said and began to laugh a little through his tears. "That was just such a nice thing you did. I absolutely love it," he finished, trying to smile as he wiped away his tears.

Emma smiled at the comment. "I'm glad you like it."

"I just feel bad. This blanket is so beautiful and well made. It must have cost quite a bit of money and probably took days."

She laughed. "People give me money from time to time. Usually I use it on food, but I decided to get a few things to knit. Don't worry, they weren't much. The blanket did take a long time, but I love knitting. After the second time you took me to eat, I decided you could use a blanket. I didn't know if I would see you again, but I thought I would at least try."

He grinned as the tears faded. "That may be the nicest thing anyone has ever done for me. Thank you, Emma," Ayden replied to the older homeless woman.

"I am the one who should be thanking you. You have done so much for me and I can never thank or repay you enough. So thank you, Ayden," Emma said, truly grateful.

Ayden shook his head while thinking back to a recurring thought he had been having. He wondered if she would ever try to see her son again. He couldn't imagine having to give up a child, and he knew it had to be hard for her.

Emma could tell Ayden was thinking something. "Is something wrong?" she asked.

He didn't say anything for a moment. "Well," he said, then paused. "I was just wondering if maybe you wanted to see your son? I just know it has to be so hard to know he's there, but doesn't know his mother. I could go with you for support if you needed it. I don't want to overstep a boundary; I just really feel your struggle," he finished and regretted what he said as soon as he finished. He knew she wouldn't like his suggestion. Who would?

Emma's face quickly transformed to a clear expression of sadness. She didn't say anything for a long while.

"Ayden, I have thought about going back to the orphanage to see him every day since I left him there," she let out and began to cry.

He knew he shouldn't have said it now. He reached down to put his hand on her shoulder for support. He wished Claire were at his side, because she would know how to make it better. Maybe then, both of them wouldn't be so sad. "I'm sorry. I didn't mean to bring it up. Please forgive me," he said trying to shrug it off.

"No. You are right. I should go to the orphanage. It has been six years of contemplating. I've never quite been able to bring myself to do it. Thanks to your support, I think I might have the strength to see him," she said through her tears.

Ayden was astonished by her response. He knew he'd overstepped the line. He expected her to be upset, which she rightfully should be. "Okay," he said enthusiastically.

He helped her to gather her composure. He gave her the support she needed, then grabbed his blanket and her bags and made his way to the car with Emma.

They arrived at the orphanage a few miles later. After a pep talk, and nearly backing out, they exited the Ford Explorer and walked in. The building was a two story townhouse that actually looked like a decent place to live. They were greeted at the front desk by a younger man.

"How can I help you today?" the man asked kindly.

Ayden looked over at Emma, who seemed to be at a loss of words. "This is the mother of one of the boys. We were hoping to visit her son," Ayden replied firmly, hoping there wouldn't be any trouble.

"Well we will have to fill out some paper work and get approval from the coordinator," the man replied back. Emma stood shyly, still silent. "Who is the son?" he continued.

The man clearly could tell the woman was homeless. He took her as one who either didn't talk, or didn't talk normally. Most people associated the homeless as having something wrong, even if a lot of them didn't, like Emma.

Ayden realized that it seemed like a lot of work and judging by Emma's reaction, she didn't want to do it all. She seemed like at any instant she would just run out.

"His name is Jackson," Emma said quietly.

"Ah, yes. Jackson. Well if you would like we can start the paperwork and I can grab the coordinator," the man said grabbing papers.

Emma looked at Ayden and shook her head. He could feel her discomfort.

"Actually I'm not sure about that. Could we maybe just get a look at him? It can be from the window. His mother just wants to see how he is," Ayden said trying not to let Emma leave while attempting to tug on an emotional string of the receptionist.

He seemed to think about it for a moment. "Fine. Follow me," he said then stood, leading them toward the window.

Ayden led Emma behind the man. They approached a window overlooking the next room. In the room it was clearly visible that a few children were playing. There were two children—a girl and a boy who couldn't have been more than three. There was a girl probably five years old, and two eight or nine year old boys. An older woman played with them and a train in the corner. On the left side sat a little boy with brown curly hair playing with Lego's. Immediately Emma's eyes were drawn to him. He appeared to be about a six year old boy. Ayden assumed that he had to be Jackson. Emma began to cry.

"That one is Jackson," the man said as he pointed toward the boy playing with Lego's. They had each guessed right.

Emma cried, and Ayden couldn't help but let a tear fall. It was difficult watching her gaze at her son that she'd been forced to give up. She had gone through so much and he knew it had to be tough looking at her son from behind a window.

They continued to watch as Jackson played alone with his Lego's.

Ayden thought about how he and Claire had wanted children. They probably would have tried for one within the next couple months. They had worked to build stability enough to raise children. Now, that would never happen. Ayden didn't ask Emma if she wanted to fill out the papers to see her son. He knew this was hard enough. Maybe eventually she would, but this was a huge step for now. He watched as she cried with simultaneous sadness and joy as she looked to her son.

Chapter 20

As new days approached, his life was ending before his eyes. His doctor had told him to go into the office, but he didn't see the point. If he was going to die, there was nothing he could do. He would hopefully be reunited with Claire soon anyways. The thought made thinking of death much easier to cope with. As easy as it was to mope and stay sad, he tried many times to think of his father's advice. It did sound nice to try to make some sort of difference with the short time he had left. He hoped that helping Emma counted. If only there was something he could do to help her more. He also wanted to do more for her son and all of those other homeless people he caroled to. There was only so much time left, and he really didn't know how much he was capable of doing, especially considering his mood was normally full of sadness, sorrow, despair, and sometimes even hate.

The day passed as rain fell outside as the Christmas season was in full swing outside his door. He had been doing all he could not long ago with Claire to add to the season, but now he just wanted it over. It all reminded him of her.

The pains were back too. They hadn't been present for the last few days. Maybe they had been masked by his constant pain from sorrow and grieving. These were the pains he had felt a couple weeks ago when he decided to get them tested. If only Claire had known he had cancer. Again he thought it was probably better that she never found out. The only person who knew was Ben. Ben promised not to say anything to anyone, which was just how Ayden wanted it. He didn't want anyone to have to deal with more heartache over him than there already was. The cancer was also something that Emma didn't know about him. Now that they were becoming friends, he wondered if he should tell the poor homeless woman. For now he decided it was his secret.

He stayed indoors through the constant rain and pain. He put the blanket Emma made for him over his body as he tried to stay warm.

**

Wednesday passed and Thursday came. Christmas was getting closer as still, he didn't embrace the season.

He met up with Emma at her usual location; Christmas in the Park. The rain had ceased for now and the sun was out yet again. The sun was unusual for a Washington winter's day. They put her belongings into the car so that no one would take them, then decided to stroll through the park.

The stroll reminded Ayden of when he had first met Claire. The night had been so magical and forever life-changing.

For the most part, they stayed quiet. Emma wore her same new jacket, jeans and shoes. Ayden was glad to see it. He wore his pea coat and jeans to try to stay warm in the crisp air.

They talked about old Christmas memories and both of their spouses. Of course Emma's memories weren't as fond as Ayden's, but they talked about them nonetheless.

Out of the corner of his eye, Ayden recognized something. He did a quick double take, trying to realize what he recognized. Then the thought popped into his head. The man was wearing the leather jacket that Emma wanted to give to her friend.

Emma waved to the man as they approached. He was clearly homeless as well, standing with another man and woman near some trees.

"Hey, Emma!" they all called over to her. She waved and smiled.

"Hey guys," she called back but didn't stop to talk.

Quickly Ayden realized they were all homeless. He also noticed the beanie and candles. They each held a candle. Ayden couldn't help but laugh watching them hold candles burning in broad daylight. He was glad to see that Emma gave out the gifts and that they had gone to good use. She really was a nice, giving person. What homeless person thinks of giving to others? They continued walking as Ayden smiled at the thought.

They talked about how she handed out the gifts and how grateful everyone was. Her best friend cried when she got the necklace. Emma had told her about Ayden and the woman replied by calling him an angel. The comment made Ayden happy as he felt maybe he was making a difference in his last days on Earth.

They continued through the Christmas trees and decorations of the park. Soon they were back at his car.

"Ayden, thank you for helping me go to the orphanage two days ago. That really helped me," she said softly as they finished their walk.

"I'm glad you got to see him," Ayden replied, as he thought of how his wife would have been jealous of Jackson.

"I was wondering if maybe we could go back?" Emma asked.

Ayden was surprised by the request. "Of course," he said enthusiastically.

Chapter 21

Not long after, they arrived again down the road at the same townhouse with letters on the outside displaying the fact it was an orphanage.

They walked up the steps and inside. The same young man greeted them from behind a desk.

"Hello, again. Merry Christmas," the man said kindly.

"Merry Christmas," Ayden replied, knowing Emma was still going through a hard emotional rollercoaster by being at the orphanage. "We were hoping to visit with Jackson today. We will fill out the papers if need be."

"Perfect. I will get the supervisor for approval." He slid the paperwork across the desk for them to fill out, then left into the next room. Emma stood back shyly. Ayden wondered curiously if she knew how to read and write. She did seem to have a somewhat normal life until her husband had left her with nothing. He knew it was wrong to wonder, but he, like many people, had a predetermined opinion of what the homeless were like.

Emma approached the paperwork, and began to fill it out. An elderly woman came out with the receptionist and greeted Emma and Ayden.

They spoke for a moment, then the woman gave the approval. She had given Emma a strange look at first;

obviously realizing she was homeless. She seemed to feel bad for Emma as she quickly approved the visit though.

They finished the paperwork, then the receptionist led them to the door to the next room.

She stood behind Ayden, seeming to be conflicted.

"Are you ready?" Ayden asked hoping to give her the support she needed to continue. She nodded. "Okay, I will wait out here then," he said, knowing this was something she needed to do on her own.

She stayed put for a long while as the young man opened the door. Finally she walked in.

Ayden watched from behind the window as Emma approached the same little boy with curly brown hair he recognized from the day before. Today he was coloring in a coloring book on a small kid-sized table.

Emma approached. The door stayed open so Ayden could hear all that was going on in the room. It seemed to be pretty noisy from the kids just playing. He watched as she weakly approached the child, wiping away her tears.

"Hello Jackson," Emma said softly as she sat next to the child coloring in a coloring book.

"Hi," the boy replied kindly then went back to coloring.

She seemed unsure of how to proceed. "What are you coloring?" she asked.

"It's a Christmas Tree," he replied in his young voice.

"It's really good," she continued, watching him color. Tears began to fall from her eyes yet again.

"Thanks," Jackson said. He still had no idea who the woman was, but she couldn't help but notice how polite he was for just a six-year-old boy. They sat in silence as she watched him color the tree with his crayons.

Ayden couldn't help but let a tear fall as he watched Emma gaze at her son. He was pretty sure she wouldn't tell the boy who she was, but he was glad to see her reunited with her son. He thought of how hard it must have been.

Chapter 22

There was one week left which also meant one week till Christmas. It was one week till his life would come to an end. Time was so slow yet so fast. Most of his days passed full of sulking, sorrow, sadness, and self-contemplation. He truly enjoyed staying to himself while thinking of Claire. Hopefully they would meet again in heaven in a week. His doctor had told him to come in, but yet another day passed and he still had no intention of going in. He was going to die of his cancer and that was all there was to it. It seemed a sure thing now that his pains were coming more and more frequently.

The phone rang and he quickly reached for it, now hoping it was Emma. His new friend did add a bit of joy to his life with the constant missing of Claire. He also wanted to help as much as he could by listening to his father's advice.

"Hello?" Ayden asked.

"Hey, man. It's Ben. How are you doing?" the friendly familiar voice replied.

"Hey, man. Holding up. How about you?" Ayden answered, not in the mood to talk about how he really was feeling.

"I am doing well. Just wanted to see if you wanted to hang tonight? Just you and me?"

"Sure man. Sounds good. Want to come over?" he said, again deciding to try to do something with his life rather than sulking, which he had already done for most the day.

"Perfect," Ben said then they hung up. Ayden went upstairs to change and get ready to hang out with his friend. He figured he only had one week left, so why not hang out with his best friend?

The phone rang again, and assuming it was Ben just forgetting to say something, he picked it up again.

"Hello?" he answered again waiting for Ben's voice.

"Hello Ayden. This is Beth. You're mother-in-law," the elderly feminine voice replied.

This was one of the last people Ayden had expected to hear from. Sure they had always had a good relationship, but they were never that close. Ayden and Claire would go to her parents' place once every month or two, but her mother never called to just talk. The last time he had seen her had been at the funeral, but they hadn't spoken. He wondered what she could possibly be calling for.

"Hello Beth. How are you?" he replied with a bit of enthusiasm to make a decent impression. She probably assumed he was still a wreck, which he truthfully was.

"Not so great, actually. Since Claire passed, I haven't been able to do much except sit on my bed crying. Frank is back working and doing okay, but I don't understand how. I just wanted to see how you were holding up through it all." He could tell she had been crying.

He wondered how he should answer and what she needed to hear. "Well to be honest, I have done a lot of sitting, and thinking. A lot of crying too. It's nearly impossible knowing she is gone." He hesitated for a moment, not knowing how to proceed. "Then I found out I have cancer," he said. It felt good to finally tell someone other than Ben. "The cancer has helped but maybe not in the way you are thinking. It's easier knowing that I will be reunited with her soon. I am not saying this is good, but it has helped me to open my eyes. Life is a fragile thing, and we should do everything we can while we are here on Earth. So I have been looking to try to make a difference with the time I have left," he said, hoping his words would help Claire's mother.

"Ayden. I am so sorry. How long do you have?" she said anxiously.

"About a week left," he said honestly.

"No! Ayden no! I am so sorry. What can I do?" she asked with obvious sadness.

"Nothing. Honestly, like I said, it's helping me to deal with Claire. I also enjoy trying to do good things. Lately I have been helping the homeless a lot. It really has helped. The way to move forward is to occupy your time with things that really do make a difference," he said hoping she understood what he was saying.

She stayed silent for a long while. "You know Ayden, you are right. Claire has shown me that life could end at any moment. I think what you are doing and how you are holding up with cancer is beautiful."

He appreciated the compliment. "Thank you Beth."

They continued talking for a few more moments about Claire, the cancer and moving on. Ayden never expected to be supporting someone else who needed to move on. He was still messed up from Claire's death. Most of his time was filled with sulking and sorrow. Now he was trying to help her mother cope. Hopefully he had helped in some way.

Another hour passed and Ben came over. They sat on the couch and turned on the basketball game. The last time Ayden had turned on the television was the night he had argued with Claire about watching a Christmas movie or going to her parents.

They watched the game as they talked a bit. They talked about the cancer and how he felt. They talked about how much Ayden missed Claire. They talked about the homeless woman and how he felt maybe he could make a difference. Then the conversation turned to Myla. Ben really seemed to like her, and Ayden was glad they had finally gotten together. They had known each other for so long. Ben mentioned that he thought she could be the one. They talked for hours, just reminiscing and watching the game. It was almost like the guy's nights they used to have before Claire's death. Back then, Myla and Claire would hang out while Ben and Ayden did as well. Those were the days. They enjoyed their night together as friends just talking. Although he thought about Claire nearly every moment, he did not cry. Sometimes you feel like being by yourself, but sometimes the company of a friend is what you really need.

Chapter 23

Saturday marked the weekend before Christmas. To Ayden, it now meant less than one week left. He thought of all that he and Claire had been able to do a couple weeks ago at just the beginning of the Christmas season. From Thanksgiving, to Black Friday shopping, to putting up lights, to practicing carols, to playing in the snow. He loved her so much.

Ayden thought of all they had done and decided that maybe he would try to enjoy the remainder of the Christmas season. It was time to get a tree. At least he would have something to stare at when he sat on the couch thinking about Claire. It would make her happy to know they at least had a Christmas tree to follow their past years' traditions.

Ayden drove down the road in his silver Ford Explorer. The clouds were out, but still no rain or snow. The day did have a wintery feel with the chill in the air. He decided that before he went, he would stop to see if Emma was there.

He drove up to Christmas in the Park. The trees were not yet lit seeing as it was daylight still. There were many people strolling through the park, clearly enjoying their holiday season.

He rounded the corner to find Emma in her normal spot. She sat on the ground, completely awake unlike most days.

She smiled weakly as she noticed Ayden. "Hey Emma. How are you today?"

"Hey Ayden, I'm still kicking. How about you?"

He laughed. "Still kicking too." He felt it was ironic that really he wouldn't be kicking much longer. "I was wondering if you might want to help me pick out a Christmas tree? Claire would want me to have one in the house," he said trying not to tear up thinking about Claire.

She thought for a moment. "Sounds great."

They drove down the street with all of Emma's belongings in the back seat. She still looked dirty, tired, and weak wearing the same clothes he had got her days prior. He wore his jeans and green jacket, trying to prepare for the soon-to-come rain or snow.

Soon enough they arrived at the tree lot. Numerous lush, green trees were spread throughout a lot. Wood chips lined the rows upon rows of trees. Ayden and Emma walked up and down aisles, observing the tall, small, large, short, fat, thin, dense, sparse, dry, lush, green, silver-lined, and many other types of Christmas trees.

Emma pointed out a few that looked nice. They compared them while making small talk. Ayden thought about whether or not to bring something up, but he didn't want to offend her. He just wanted her to have a better life.

"Emma," he said deciding to bring it up after all. "I was wondering if maybe you would let me help you find a place to stay," he said, knowing the reaction probably wouldn't go well.

She looked up. "Thank you Ayden, but no thank you." He knew that would probably happen and he didn't want to push her further. He just didn't know how she could live without her own place. He at least wanted her to stay at the shelter.

"I understand," he said. If there was anything he learned from Claire, it was that women are always right, even when they are wrong. He loved that Claire always challenged him. The thought made him miss her more.

They continued comparing the trees. Finally they found a tree about seven feet tall; very full and extremely green. They purchased it, then Ayden strapped it onto his roof.

Suddenly a burst of pain hit his back. He jumped down and held his back in agony. He realized Emma was watching.

She came over quickly. "Are you okay Ayden? What happened?" she asked.

He got up trying to mask the pain, hoping it would subside soon. "Oh nothing. I'm fine."

The pain began to fade and Emma seemed to buy his lie for the time being. They got into the car.

"Would you like to help me decorate it?" he asked hoping she wouldn't take it the wrong way by inviting her to his house. They truly were just friends. Nothing more. They really were like brother and sister.

"I would love to," she said in her soft voice. At her words, they headed down the road back to his house.

They arrived at his modern-style suburban home, decorated with the lights and decorations he and his wife had put up a couple weeks ago. He hoped she wouldn't be uncomfortable. He felt bad, realizing he had so much more than she did.

"This is a beautiful home. The type I always hoped to have with my husband," she said as they got out of the car.

"Thank you. Claire wanted a home like this, so of course we got one. I do love it too," he said still hoping she would handle being at his home okay.

They walked into the house. To Ayden, it was routine and ordinary. Emma seemed taken aback by everything though. She began to let her eyes wander, looking around the home.

"This is really nice," she said, taking in the carpet and crown molding with light tan walls. She looked into the living room with its elegant couches and flat screen television. The stairs led up to more rooms. Then she looked over at the picture hung on the wall. It was Ayden with a beautiful woman next to him smiling.

"She is so pretty, Ayden," she said. He looked over at the picture. Since her death, he hadn't really been able to bring himself to look at the picture. It was just too hard. Ayden pushed back tears as he looked at his beautiful wife by his side. She was the most beautiful woman in the world.

"She really was," he replied through his tears. They stared at the picture for a long while. Finally, he composed himself enough to move on.

He moved a coffee table out of the way of the living room, then got his tree stand out of the garage. They attached it to the tree then carried it into the living room.

The seven-foot, full, lush, green tree looked great. It would add to Ayden's holiday spirit that for the past couple weeks had been non-existent.

"Well, shall we decorate?" he asked. Emma nodded and he went to retrieve the box of ornaments and lights from the garage. She hesitated from sitting on the elegant couch. She knew she was dirty and truly did not want to mess anything up in the perfect house. She hadn't been in a house so nice before, even though it would probably be considered a middle class home. Even when she wasn't homeless, she hadn't ever been well off. She decided to stand so that she wouldn't let her dirtiness affect the home.

Ayden came back and they strung the lights. They talked about Christmas memories and Claire. He didn't bring up Jackson as he knew it was still a touchy subject. He was glad she had even agreed to go visit him. Ayden knew that was a huge step. They talked and enjoyed each other's company while putting up the ornaments.

Many of the ornaments were from Claire. She had either bought them or had them from her childhood. The memories swarmed in as they hung the decorations.

Suddenly it happened. The shattering noise rattled through the house. They each looked down wide-eyed. The broken glass was scattered all over the hard wood floor.

Emma had dropped an ornament. Ayden knew this wasn't just any ornament. It was the first ornament he and Claire had bought on their first Christmas married together. On it were both of their names: Claire and Ayden. The ornament had been the most important of any.

Ayden stared in shock. "I am so, so sorry," she said pleading for forgiveness.

"It's okay," Ayden said. He felt a sense of peace. The ornament did bring memories, but it was just an ornament. He hated seeing Emma so sad on his behalf.

She looked up to see if his reaction was truly genuine. It was. They both picked up the pieces. He reassured her it was okay.

They continued making memories of their own, decorating the tree in his living room. Christmas spirit seemed to be coming back to Ayden now with the help of his new homeless friend, Emma.

When they finished putting up all the ornaments, they got back into the car to take Emma and her belongings back.

"Are you sure I can't help you get a place to stay?" he asked as he pulled out of his garage and into the dark night. He suddenly realized that snow was hitting the windshield. It wasn't too hard yet, but it was still snow. He really didn't want her sleeping in it again.

He looked over to find that Emma was staring at the snow. Maybe she would finally change her mind. "Like I said, no thank you," she said firmly.

He decided not to push it further even though he felt he had a moral responsibility to at least try. They drove back toward Christmas in the Park.

Soon they saw the endless trees and bright lights and decorations of the park. The sight was still breathtaking as always. Emma smiled as she saw it with the snow falling to cover the trees to create a beautiful holiday scene, just like something out of a movie.

They arrived, and Ayden reluctantly got her belongings to help her to her normal spot. He felt bad that he was letting her sleep out in the freezing snowy night. It was her decision though.

She leaned in for a friendly hug. "Enjoy your tree. I always love looking at all of mine," she said. He realized she meant the ones here in the park. He smiled.

"Thanks for your help, Emma. Let me know if you change your mind about a place to stay, you have my card.

Have a good night," he said to her as she prepared for her night.

"Your wife is watching over you. She is a beautiful person. Goodnight, Ayden," she replied then climbed into her sleeping bag. Walking away, Ayden shivered in the cold snow.

He wondered what prompted her to say that. Whatever it was, he appreciated it. He hoped Claire was watching over him. He couldn't stop thinking about her.

He drove back down the road slowly, trying to stay safe in the snow. He really wished he would have convinced Emma not to sleep out in the snow. He knew she had an emotional tie to the spot in Christmas in the Park she stayed at, but it was still saddening.

Suddenly he swerved. He'd been blindsided by unbearable pain. The car slid through the ice and off the road. He slammed on his breaks just as the car began to slide to its side. The car slammed forward into a pile of snow in a sudden impact.

The pain was incredible. Ayden held his back trying to regain his composure. The car had run off the road but he realized he was okay. Luckily he noticed that he hadn't hit anything but snow. The crash could have been much worse. Anxiety rushed through his body from the sudden impact. He cringed from the pain. This had definitely been the most agonizing physical pain he had experienced in all his life.

He sat in the car a long while, as his back felt as though it was ripping apart. He cried from the tremendous pain. He wanted it gone.

Nearly half an hour passed and he sat in the car. Not one car had passed him on the street as the snow fell harder. He couldn't see out of his windshield as the snow seemed to be blanketing the car. He knew this could become a very dangerous situation. His pain was just too unbearable to drive. If he wanted to make it back, he needed to leave soon. He let out a long scream from the pain.

The pain was the only thing he could think of.

Then the thought came to him, and he decided he needed to do it. "Dear Heavenly Father." He hadn't prayed since his wife had passed. At times he was too angry that God had taken his wife. He knew that if he wanted to make it to heaven, though, that was not what he should be doing. "Please help me. I don't know what to do and the pain is so bad. Please Lord. I have been through so much and it is all just so hard. Please!" he said and began weeping. The pain was nearly unbearable and the snow fell harder and harder.

Then, the pain began to fade. He could move his back. Feeling was coming back to him. Instantly he knew his prayer had been answered and he started his car. He put on the windshield wipers and tried backing out.

The car slipped at first as the tires seemed to be moving in place. Then they caught traction and reversed onto the road. He continued using the wipers to move the snow off the windshield. He could see out of a small portion, and decided to just drive cautiously.

The pain was now completely gone. The wipers knocked more snow off as he continued home, alone. He hoped that his last week alive would not consist of more pain like that. Maybe it was time to visit the doctor. He drove down, thinking of how thankful he was to have the pain gone. He also knew his wife was watching over him from above. Tears fell, as he loved her so much.

Chapter 24

Sunday came and went. He debated on going to church, as last Sunday he had gone with Emma. He couldn't bring himself to go with the near constant pain though. The pain was back. He lay in bed all day, trying to stay strong enough through it. He knew it was time to go to the doctor, but the pain was too much to even move. He wished Claire were there to help him. Whenever he had been sick, she had always nursed him back to health. She was always so giving and loving. He wondered if Emma went to church without him and he hoped she had stayed warm through the snow even though he knew she most likely had not.

***

Monday came and there were only four days left till Christmas and the end of Ayden's life. He stayed up nearly all night, and this time it wasn't just from dreading being without Claire. This time his physical pain was so overwhelming that he couldn't get more than an hour of sleep.

When seven in the morning approached, he decided it was time to see his doctor. He mustered enough strength to drive down to his doctor's office.

Hours passed while he waited again in the office. He paced back and forth, read a magazine, and mostly thought of Claire. He took a few tests and waited for his doctor to deliver the results. To his relief, the pain had faded ironically in the doctor's office.

"Mr. Johnson," Dr. Phillips finally called, and he walked back following him into a patient's room.

"I'm afraid I am not sure what is going on. I still see the cancer, but now it looks not as progressed as before. The odd thing is that your pains shouldn't be this strong yet. Basically, the cancer and your pains don't add up. The look of the cancer now almost appears as though it has shrunk. Therapy is looking like a much better option at this point. Nonetheless, I don't want to get your hopes up. This could be a misreading," the doctor said in his white coat and tousled brown hair.

Ayden tried to process all that he was saying. His pains were more advanced than the stage his cancer was at. His cancer may be diminishing? Was he going to die? Endless unanswered questions swarmed through his head.

"Am I still going to die?" Ayden asked.

The doctor hesitated. "I'm sorry Ayden, but in my opinion, yes. I don't know what to make of your results today, but the results before were certain you had till around Christmas. If the results are correct and the cancer is lessening, you never know. At least you would have more time to live at that. I really don't know. I suggest we try therapy anyways and maybe take some more tests tomorrow."

"Tests? So I might not die on Christmas?" he asked anxiously.

"Ayden I really don't know. Your pains suggest it may be sooner, but the tests suggest you have much longer. I suggest that you stay for overnight observation. You will have better care here."

Ayden thought about it and quickly decided that if he really only had till Christmas, or even less time than that, he didn't want to live the rest of it in the hospital.

"With all due respect, doctor, if I only have a couple days left, I don't want to spend them in the hospital," Ayden said, feeling overwhelmed.

"I understand. Come in tomorrow and we can run more tests and try therapy," Dr. Phillips replied calmly.

Ayden left for home, still free from pain. He didn't know what to think after his doctor's words. His pains suggested he had less time to live, but his results showed the cancer was going away? What could be happening? All he knew was if he did have till Christmas, then he didn't want to stay in the hospital. He wished Claire were with him for the comfort and support he needed. He was also glad that she wasn't so that she wouldn't have to deal with the worry and pain.

Chapter 25

Tuesday came and Ayden decided it was at least time to tell his work he wouldn't be coming back soon. He wanted to let them know of his situation and why he didn't know when he would be back. If he really only had a couple days left, why would he work? If the test results were correct, however, and he did have much longer, he wanted to have a fall back.

Luckily for him, his boss was more than supportive. He offered to help in any way necessary. Ben had already told him about his wife and that he was sick, but Ben hadn't mentioned the cancer. Ayden appreciated him keeping the secret. He really was a great friend.

Hours of loneliness and sulking passed as Ayden stared at the Christmas tree he and Emma had put up. There had been the incident of her dropping the ornament, but he was okay with it. It was distressing at first, but it was more saddening to see Emma upset over what she had done. There was no need to be upset, especially with a homeless woman who had a harder life than he could ever imagine.

He decided to go see her. He knew a new Christmas comedy was playing in theaters, and he wondered if she might want to go. He and Claire had always been a fan of the movies and tried to go a couple times a month. He knew the movie was one that Claire wanted to see. The thought was depressing, but he would still try to heed his father's advice and do all he could with his life if he really did only have a couple days. If he did have longer as the results suggested, he knew that life should be about making a difference, any way he could.

He approached Christmas in the Park, which was now lit as the sky was dark and clear. He wore a beanie and his black pea coat to stay warm from the harsh chill. He parked and walked through the Christmas trees to the entrance.

A smile struck his face when he saw the same older homeless woman, still dirty, but wearing the clothes he had given her. She noticed him immediately.

"Hey, Ayden," she said. Their visits were becoming more regular now, even though he hadn't seen her in a couple days.

"Hey, Emma. How are you?" he asked kindly as he walked up next to her sitting on the ground. He wondered how park-goers treated her. Were they mean and rude like many were to the homeless?

"I'm okay. What are you doing?" she asked in her soft, tired voice. She looked just as dirty as usual, with her same matted hair.

"Well, I was wondering if you might want to go see a Christmas movie at the theater?" he asked.

She thought for a moment. "I haven't been to the movies since my husband left."

Ayden thought about what her life must really be like. He and Claire had gone every month. Six years without the luxury of going to a movie? Her life was unreal to him. She was a stronger person than he could ever be.

"Okay," she finally said as he waited for her reply.

"Great." They grabbed her stuff and headed out of the lit park of Christmas decorations and trees toward the car.

***

Emma and Ayden waited outside the movie theater for tickets to the wildly popular Christmas comedy. As he expected, they received many odd looks. Many looks were judgmental and some were full of hate. Ayden wished he could tell the people to stop it. He wished he could get them to realize she was a person too. She had dealt with so much, and scrutinizing looks should not be another thing on the list. He didn't know how some people could be so heartless and unsympathetic.

They got their tickets and sat down in the immaculate movie theater. He noticed that Emma was taking it all in. People looked at her and him strangely as it was still clear she was a homeless woman. He was glad she decided to go. He could use a laugh. He wished Claire was by his side to laugh with him, but that wasn't a reality anymore.

Crowds filled the theater for what appeared to be a sold out show. One empty seat sat next to him on the corner of an aisle.

From the corner, an older man most likely in his eighties hobbled up the stairs with a hunch. Ayden looked over as he noticed the man was struggling up the stairs alone. He was using a cane in one hand and his other hand against the railing for balance. The man clearly was alone. There were nearly no seats left.

Out of instinct, Ayden got up. He walked down the steps till he met the man. The man continued to hobble forward.

"Excuse me, sir. There is an open seat next to me. Could I help you up?" Ayden asked, surprising himself.

115

Normally he would feel bad and wish there was something he could do in a situation like this, but his emotions led him to want to help the elderly, lonely man.

The man looked up with an aged half smile. "Thank you, sir," he said. He reached out his arm for support and Ayden held his arm around him to help him walk up the stairs. Hundreds of people continued to sit and chat in the dimly-lit theater, for the most part no one paying attention to Ayden and the elderly man.

A few rows up and Ayden led him to the seat. "Thank you. You are very kind," the old man said in a raspy voice. They exchanged smiles and relaxed into the theater seats. Ayden looked over to see Emma smiling at his deed.

The thought was sad to him that this old man, who could barely get around, was by himself in the movie. Ayden had never gone to the movies alone, and he wondered how it would feel. He knew it was probably lonely. He wondered what the man's story was. Maybe his wife had passed too.

Suddenly a sharp pain hit his back. He jolted forward and held his spine. Emma had clearly noticed. He tried to relax as the pain quickly went away. While it had lasted, though, it felt as though a knife had stabbed into him.

"What's wrong?" Emma asked anxiously.

"Oh, nothing. It went away," he said trying to reassure her. She stared at him for a moment then relaxed back into her seat. The pain was gone for now and he hoped it wouldn't be back. He sat back as well.

The movie started and the entire theatre enjoyed the well-done Christmas comedy. Ayden tried to concentrate and enjoy it, and occasionally he did. He laughed and tried to take it all in. For the most part however, he was lost in thought. He thought about Claire and his parents. He thought about his dad's words and also wondered how Claire's mother was doing. He thought of Ben and Myla. He thought about Emma and her son. He thought about the elderly man next to him. He wished there was more he could do. He watched and thought, as the movie went on, with Emma on one side and the elderly man on the other.

The movie ended and everyone clapped. Emma smiled brightly. Ayden offered to help the old man back to his car. He agreed thankfully and they slowly walked together down the stairs and out the theater. Emma followed behind them.

They made it out to an old beat up Honda in the parking lot. He felt bad that this was the car that the old man drove. He wished there was more he could do for the man as he probably had a lonely life.

"You are a very kind young man. Thank you, sir. Merry Christmas," the old man said in his raspy voice as he climbed into his car.

"Merry Christmas, sir. Thank you," Ayden replied. He felt good to have helped him. He and Emma headed back. Again she refused a place to stay and again he wasn't going to push it further.

They said goodnight and he dropped her off at her home—Christmas in the Park. Ayden drove off down the road; alone and lonely yet again. Life was not the same without Claire.

Chapter 26

Ring Ring Ring. Ring Ring Ring. Ayden woke to the sudden burst of noise from the phone. The light was barely visible outside as he turned to his alarm clock to find it was only seven a.m. In a dreary state, he picked up the phone.

"Hello?" he asked groggily into the phone.

"Hey, Ayden. This is Emma," said the weak woman's voice on the other end of the line.

"Hey, Emma. What's up?" Ayden asked with sleep still in his voice. He wondered if something was wrong since she was calling so early in the morning.

"Will you take me to the orphanage today? I want to tell Jackson I am his mother," she said firmly as if she had rehearsed the line.

"Of course. How about noon?" He was shocked at her request, but it made him happy. Maybe he really was doing some good with his life.

"Thank you, Ayden."

They hung up and Ayden smiled as he thought about her request. He decided to get up, but before he would pick up Emma, he had one other thing he wanted to do first.

He looked over to the other side of the bed where Claire normally laid. The spot was empty. His heart sunk yet again, but he tried to shrug it off, then got up and ready.

***

Ayden drove out of his unlit decorated home in his silver Ford Explorer with a goal in mind. He contemplated on where to go exactly, but he drove on a mission.

He went into the mall filled with enormous crowds, rushing with life. He came out after finding what he needed then waiting in a line that took almost an hour. He was determined.

Noon came and Ayden parked at Christmas in the Park as Emma walked toward the car. She waved and put her bags in the back. Something was different about Emma. She was wearing the church dress he had gotten her. She looked nicer than Ayden was used to. He was glad she was getting use out of it. He figured she wanted to make a good impression. She had her hair in a ponytail, probably trying to hide the fact her hair was matted and dirty. She still looked dirty and homeless, but to some she might be able to pass as a normal woman.

"You look nice, Emma," he said, complimenting his friend. "Thank you. I've been pretty nervous all day," she replied anxiously.

He noticed her hand shaking. He reached into the back to pull out a giant set of Lego's. The Lego's had been the gift he was determined to get earlier at the mall.

Her mouth opened wide in shock. "This is for you to give Jackson," he said, hoping she wouldn't take it the wrong way.

She seemed unsure how to respond, then finally she smiled. "Thank you Ayden. That was really nice of you," she replied in her soft voice.

They drove down the road past Christmas in the Park toward the orphanage.

Inside they were greeted by the same young man from behind the desk. He led them back to the next room.

"I'll wait out here. He will love you Emma. Don't be nervous," Ayden said as he stood still behind the window.

She nodded, holding the giant box of Lego's in her hand. He noticed her hands still shaking as she was obviously fluttering with nerves. Ayden wondered how he would handle a situation like this. If only he would have been able to have a child with Claire. It would be an experience he would never know.

Ayden watched as she walked in. Again it was loud as the children were all playing. In the corner by himself was the same curly-haired boy in a red polo shirt. He sat on the floor playing with Lego's. The homeless woman in the church dress walked toward him hesitantly.

"Hey, Jackson," she said. Jackson looked up at her, remembering her face from the day before. Ayden wondered if her homely appearance fazed him at all.

"Hello," he answered kindly yet again and went back to his Lego's.

"I was hoping to talk to you," she said, speaking slowly. Jackson looked up again.

"About what?" he asked curiously. He eyed the giant box in her hand.

"Well first, these are for you," she said, handing the giant box of Lego's over to him. His eyes didn't move even for a second as his jaw dropped.

"Wow!" he said as he took them reluctantly. "Lego's! Thank you!" he said in his childish voice. Ayden wondered if he ever got gifts in the orphanage.

"Jackson. I'm your mother," she said. Emma seemed relieved but unsure the moment she said it. A tear fell from her eye. "I am so sorry this is the first time I told you," she said, crying harder.

The boy looked blindsided. He was stunned and shocked; seeming speechless. "Am I going to have a home?" was all he said.

She began crying harder. Ayden knew that question would hurt. He immediately felt as though it was all his fault.

"Maybe someday, Jackson," she said after a long pause. Her tears flowed. Jackson looked unsure of what to do. He'd just got a gift. There was a strange woman who said she was his mom. And, the woman was crying.

Then, all of the sudden, the boy stood. He walked a step toward Emma and wrapped his arms around her, just barely above her waist. She bent down out of instinct and hugged the child back. She kept crying as she held her son for the first time in years.

A tear came to Ayden's eyes as the unexpected scene occurred before him. The boy accepted that Emma was his mother. The boy didn't have even a hint of anger. He didn't know how to react, but what he did know was that he might be one step closer to a home and family. He had lived in an orphanage his whole life, never being adopted. They embraced in a touching hug that signified the start of a mother and son relationship.

Chapter 27

Thursday was Christmas Eve—the day before his original predicted death. His last visit to the doctor went against that prediction however. The new advice from his doctor was that his pain suggested he had less time, which meant it could be today, or according to the tests he could have much more time, where the date was unknown. Either way, Ayden was coming to terms with the fact that he was going to die. He would hopefully have lived a righteous enough life to join Claire in heaven. He had tried his best to listen to his dad's advice. His time, for all he knew, was at its end.

For days, he felt compelled to visit his wife's gravesite before he died, but he couldn't bring himself to do it. He sat and sulked most days, and could never seem to get her out of his mind. He was constantly sad. He didn't know what would happen if he visited her grave. Today was the day he would find out.

***

Ayden arrived at Christmas in the Park on the afternoon of Christmas Eve. The air was cold and his face was numb as he walked through the park toward the entrance. More people were in the park even though it wasn't lit yet, probably because of the fact it was Christmas Eve. He wore the gray sweater that Claire had given him for Christmas the year before accompanied by jeans. He slicked back his hair the way Claire had always liked it.

Emma sat there in her normal spot, still wearing the new jacket. She had her hair up in the back like the day before when she had seen her son. Emma still looked dirty and homeless, but something about her seemed to signify hope. His newfound friend seemed happier than he had ever seen. Maybe he had made a difference.

She looked up and smiled as he approached.

"Emma, will you go with me to visit Claire's grave?" Ayden asked directly.

She seemed taken aback by the proposition. She hesitated, looking down. Ayden's heart sunk. Without the support of someone else, it would be unbearable.

"Of course," she finally said with a weak smile.

They gathered her belongings and drove off down to the gravesite.

Nerves and anxiety filled Ayden as he thought about what was to come.

In a few minutes that felt like a few hours, they were finally there at the cemetery.

Ayden knew where she would be, but as he exited the car, he looked up to the cloudy sky and was met with a bitingly cold chill against his face. He stood still looking out at the endless gravestones. It was the place where life stopped. It was also the last place he had seen his wife.

Emma approached his side with a smile for encouragement. They began to walk along the pathway that led through the cemetery.

The feeling was bleak, cold, sad and morbid. Emma was a really great friend to accompany him to his wife's burial site. He didn't know if he would have had it in him to go with a friend to visit their deceased spouse. He was grateful.

They walked for minutes past numerous trees and gravestones. The grassy plains had a few people here and there, visiting the graves of their loved ones. Not one person had a look of happiness.

After more walking, Ayden knew they were there. He led her onto the grass past a few more graves. Then they approached a fresher looking mound of grass accompanied by a grave stone.

Ayden tried his hardest to hold back the wave of tears. Grief flooded in as his heart sunk. Emma stayed respectfully silent as she knew they were at the right spot.

Then tears gushed out as he began to weep. He looked up at the bleak skies then down to the gravestone. Just beneath him was his lifeless wife. It was hard to imagine now that he would never see her again. She lay lifeless just under him. He would never see her smile, feel her touch, smell her scent, listen to her voice, or do anything with her again on Earth. She was gone and it was all his fault. Why couldn't he have just gone with her? Why? He looked at the words on her grave.

Claire Johnson.

A loving wife, daughter, and friend

A truly beautiful person

Emma stayed back as he cried, standing still. She knew his pain. She wished there was something she could do, but she knew she couldn't.

They stayed at the site as minutes passed and tears fell. Each stayed silent and still. Finally, Emma reached her hand onto Ayden's shoulder. With the feel of her touch came comfort. He needed support in his time of sadness and pain. He appreciated his friend as tears continued to fall.

Then it happened. The pain shot through his back and he fell to his knees. Ayden clutched his back as he felt nothing. The numbness hit immediately as he didn't know where he was, or what was happening. He blanked as another shot of pain hit his back. He seemed to be tearing apart from the inside. It felt like a knife ripped multiple holes and tore them further all at one time. Tears fell from his eyes as he now lay on the ground screaming. He screamed a loud screeching noise that tore apart his lungs and brought a great relief to his chest.

Emma kneeled above him. After multiple attempts, she finally got through to him. "Ayden what is wrong?" she said crying in fear. She seemed just as disoriented as Ayden.

He began to wake from his state of unbearable pain that left him in a daze.

He was at a loss for words.

"Ayden. Please," Emma pleaded for him to respond as he lay on the ground clutching his back with his eyes closed.

"My back. Hospital," he let out through his pain and tears.

"Someone call an ambulance!" she screamed to a few people who stood around the cemetery. Multiple people scrambled to their phones as everyone seemed terrified by the screams that had emerged from Ayden's mouth. He was clearly in agony.

"They are on their way!" a woman called, still on her phone.

"They are on their way, Ayden. What is the problem?" Emma asked him. Ayden opened his eyes. The pain was incredible and he knew he couldn't move. He noticed the crowd around him and the homeless woman above him; his friend Emma.

"Emma, you need to know," he said lightly, then paused. "I have cancer." As soon as he said it, relief flooded in. It felt good to finally tell her. She had the right to know from him before he died. He didn't know if he had minutes, a day, or many days, but he felt like it was coming to an end with the pain he felt now.

"What? Cancer? No. You can't. You're too young," she said in a bit of a ramble through her tears as she tried to clear her scrambled thoughts.

"I have cancer. I'm supposed to die tomorrow," he said. She had to know.

She cried unsure of how to react. "No!"

Through his pain, he could still feel her reaction. He hated causing this woman the amount of pain she appeared to be experiencing. She was his friend now. Was it wrong for him to help and befriend her when he knew he was going to die?

"I'm sorry, Emma," he said as he closed his eyes with the pain overcoming his body. He let out another horrific scream as the knife seemed to be ripping apart his insides.

Everything went black. Then a bright white light overcame everything. The light was incredible. Although it was blinding, a sense of comfort seemed to come from it. He felt the light taking over his body. Then everything was still.

Chapter 28

Emma paced back and forth through the waiting room of the hospital. She had no clue what had happened to Ayden. She hadn't cared so much about anyone in six years. Sure, she had friends whom she saw nearly every day, but there was no one else like Ayden. Of course she loved her son unconditionally, but he had taken over a different part of her heart completely. She didn't have relatives and the last person she really cared about hurt her the most. Her husband had simply left her. Now her friend was in the hospital and she didn't know if he was even alive. Cancer? Why was everything so hard for her? She finally opened herself up to someone, and she was rewarded with him dying?

"Is Emma here?" a female nurse called from the doors that opened to patient rooms.

"Yes," she shouted back full of anticipation. The nurse shot her a skeptical look, clearly noticing her homeless, dirty appearance.

"Follow me," the nurse replied emotionless.

They continued down a hall past a few rooms till finally the nurse stood in front of an open door. Emma peeked around the corner and walked in.

There he was, eyes open and still alive. Relief flooded in as she realized she hadn't lost her friend.

"Hey, Emma. Thanks for coming down," he said in the same voice she was used to. The pain must have gone away. He wore a patient's gown, but other than that, he seemed fine.

"You're okay?" she wondered out loud.

"For now. Thank you for helping me earlier," he replied calmly.

She tried to gather her fleeing thoughts. "Are you going to live?" she finally asked with a sharp tone.

He hesitated. "I honestly don't know," he said then paused. "Originally, I found out three weeks ago, and the doctor said I had till Christmas day. Then a few days ago, I had pains that suggested I may go sooner, which could mean any time now. But I also had a new set of tests that suggested I had much longer to live. So I really don't know."

She tried to take it all in. Tears fell as she thought about his response. He could die any time.

"Emma. It will be okay. All I know is for now, I feel fine," he said trying to reassure her. She sat down, still in distress.

"Emma, visiting hours are going to be up soon. I have one request," he said to her with a serious look.

"Anything."

"I want you to visit Jackson. Don't worry about me. He needs you more than I do. He really does love you and he will understand the sacrifice you made for him. Just visit him. It's Christmas Eve."

She looked into his eyes. He didn't expect her to agree, at least initially. "Okay. I will," she replied softly.

It hadn't been the reaction he had expected at all. He expected to have to make his case. To his delight she accepted. He smiled as he looked at the homely homeless woman. Her look was distressing, but the woman truly did bring hope. He was glad that maybe he had made enough of a difference to reunite a mother and her son.

"Excuse me. Visiting hours are now over," said a nurse who peeked into the door.

"Okay," Emma replied, then stood. "I need to get my belongings from your car."

"Just take the car. You can sleep in it if you'd like. Or, as always, my offer still stands to give you a room. Just bring the car back tomorrow. I will be here overnight for observation."

She laughed. "No hotel. And no it's okay; I don't even have a license. I can walk."

"Did you ever learn to drive?" Ayden wondered aloud.

"Well, yeah. I used to have a license. But when I lost my home, I lost my car too," she said sadly.

"Just take it. Please. No excuses," he said firmly.

She seemed to contemplate it as he held out the keys. He knew Emma had driven the car over to the hospital, which was why he knew she could drive.

She took the keys which left Ayden with a smile.

"Goodbye, Emma," Ayden said to her, looking into his friend's eyes.

"Goodbye, Ayden," she replied then took off out the door.

Once she was gone, Ayden pulled out a pen and nice piece of cream-colored stationary from the desk near the bed.

He pulled out a book for padding, and began to write.

Chapter 29

Emma drove down the streets of Campbell toward the orphanage. She didn't feel comfortable behind the wheel, but she would listen to Ayden's request. He was a dying man for goodness sake, what could she do? She drove by her home, the beautiful Christmas in the Park. The numerous dazzling trees were filled with never-ending lights of all sorts. People walked through the park with joy and happiness, celebrating the birth of Jesus. It was Christmas Eve, which brought joy to her heart. She loved being able to stay in the park during the Christmas season. It was so elegant and nice. She smiled as she watched Christmas in the Park disappear behind her.

Emma parked the car at the orphanage then hesitated in the driver's seat. She knew what she should do, but every time it took so much to do it. He was her son, nonetheless, and maybe someday, they would be permanently reunited. She knew it was because of Ayden that they had met again. It was Ayden who really had helped her to feel hope. He was a beautiful person, so giving and humble. She felt awful about his wife. It was clear every time she saw him that he was in deep pain. It was a pain she hoped she would never know. Now he may be leaving her. It wasn't a romantic love, but a love of friends. She didn't want him to die. The thought was devastating. She sighed heavily then exited the car and walked up to the orphanage.

She walked in and was greeted by the same young man who sat behind the desk as usual. He looked up and smiled. "Merry Christmas. Here to see Jackson?" he asked kindly.

Emma appreciated the fact the young man didn't seem to care she was homeless even though she knew it was obvious. She had the nice clothes Ayden had given her so generously, but that still didn't mask the fact she didn't have a home.

She nodded. "Merry Christmas. Yes, I am," she replied somewhat proudly.

He smiled and showed her back to the room behind them. He opened the door and she walked in. The room was noisy with the children playing. She stood at the door.

Then she saw him. Jackson softened as he saw his mother walk into the room. His curly brown hair and young face was breathtaking. He grinned up at her and she felt a tear trickle down her face. He wore a red sweater and blue jeans as he played with his new set of Lego's. She smiled at the sight.

"Hey, Jackson," she said as she walked toward him.

"Hi, Mom." He called her mom. The words triggered an emotional waterfall. She began to cry as happiness and hope filled her whole body. He had called her mom.

She sat at the table smiling at him as he smiled back. Then they began to build the Lego set together; as mother and son.

Chapter 30

Christmas Day brought with it hope and happiness. The day before had been bittersweet. Ayden had told her that he had cancer. He also had pains that scared her half to death. She didn't know how long he had left. Her new friend that brought hope and joy into her life may now be leaving it. She didn't know if she could take that, not after everything she had gone through already in her life. The sweetness came from her son Jackson. Just seeing his face made Emma smile. He symbolized a second chance and love. She loved him. He had called her Mom. The word had brought such happiness to her heart that she was left in joyful tears. She hoped that someday, maybe she would be able to care for him. Her whole life seemed to be changing, so why couldn't it continue to do so?

The Christmas season was a beautiful thing to Emma. She loved to see the spirit in the air as people generally seemed happier, more understanding, and giving. The birth of Jesus was truly a joyous event that needed to be celebrated. She never forgot what Christmas was about when it came. It filled her with hope.

This Christmas may have been filled with more hope than she ever had experienced before. The last few had sure been tough, but out of the blue Ayden came into her life and changed it all.

As she drove in Ayden's silver Ford Explorer, she couldn't help but beam as she observed the people walking with grins, wearing their new Christmas clothes.

After she had seen Jackson and played with the Lego's, she drove back to Christmas in the Park. For the first time the whole Christmas season, she hadn't slept outside in her normal spot next to her favorite tree. Instead, she parked outside and slept in the comfort of the car. It had been the warmest night she had experienced in a long time. She always sought comfort in her normal spot she felt was home, but the car brought a comfort of its own. It was warm and secure. At least she didn't have to worry about someone stealing her things, which had happened before.

Emma continued down the street toward the hospital, thinking of Christmas as "O Holy Night" played on the car stereo. The song was joyous and added to the feel of Christmas. She needed to visit Ayden and make sure his pains hadn't come back. He had mentioned something about his time being up on Christmas, but that couldn't be. He seemed okay after the pains went away, so she tried to push the thought from her head.

After she checked on Ayden she would visit her son for Christmas. Just thinking of Jackson brought a smile to her face.

She parked Ayden's car in the lot that held in it many other cars. The thought that all these people were at the hospital on Christmas Day wasn't pleasant. She hoped the patients would all at least experience some sort of Christmas today.

She was wearing the same jacket and shoes Ayden had so graciously bought for her. She tied back her hair in hopes that maybe someone wouldn't think she was homeless.

She walked into the large tinted-glass building through the sliding glass doors. Inside was the same Christmas tree in the lobby as the day before, decorated with magnificent ornaments and lights. She smiled as she looked at it. Poinsettias lined the walkway leading toward the front desk. A plump red-cheeked woman in scrubs sat at the desk staring at her computer. She obviously was making the most of the fact that she had to work rather than spend time with her family on Christmas Day. Emma felt that it was nice that people would give up their time to help others on holidays.

Emma smiled as she approached. "Merry Christmas. I am here to see Ayden Johnson," she said kindly.

"Merry Christmas. One moment," the woman replied, returning Emma's smile before looking at her computer. She began to type and then looked confused. She stared intently at her screen. Then she looked back up. She held out a finger as she picked up her phone.

Emma began to panic slightly but assumed this was probably protocol. The nurse talked into the phone quietly as Emma tried not to listen by acting preoccupied by looking outside.

"One moment, ma'am. A doctor will be right with you," the plump woman said, then looked back down at her computer.

"Thanks," Emma replied then sat at the nearest chair. She waited for minutes as her thoughts ran wild.

Then a man in a white coat and glasses came from behind the swinging doors. He looked around; probably unsure of who he was looking for. The woman behind the desk pointed toward Emma, then he followed her finger and began to walk toward her.

"Are you a relative of Mr. Johnson?" the doctor asked in an emotionless tone.

"Friend," she replied nervously as her heart pounded.

"Are you Emma?" he asked still without emotion.

"Yes," she exclaimed. "How did you know?" she wondered aloud.

"Emma. I'm afraid I have tough news to deliver. I assume you knew Mr. Johnson had cancer and it was very progressed?" he asked, looking for her reaction. She nodded, unsure of what he was getting at. "I'm afraid the cancer won. Ayden passed away in his sleep this morning. I am so sorry," he finished while looking down at the small homeless woman sitting in the chair.

Every emotion hit her at one time; fear, disbelief, uncertainty, sadness, grief, hate, anger, hurt, hopelessness, sorrow. Her heart sunk as it sped a million miles a second. Could it be real? Could any of it be real? He had just come into her life and now he was gone? He died? How could it be?

Tears gushed out as she began to weep. The grief felt like it was tearing her heart apart. He was dead? The man who had brought her such hope was dead? She cried and cried as she fell to her knees, pleading for it not to be real.

The doctor stood still as he watched the woman cry endlessly. Her loud screams and pleadings were too difficult to watch. He felt the sadness the woman was going through. He waited as she cried.

After minutes upon minutes of tears, sorrow and disbelief, the doctor spoke. "I am so sorry," he said. "Last night, before he went to sleep, he gave me this note. He told me to give it to you when you came back."

Emma looked up, trying to see through the endless warm tears that left her hollow and sunken. She looked up to find a piece of stationary in the doctor's hand reached out toward her.

She wondered what it could be. She was still in disbelief that he was dead. How could it be? The sorrow continued to rip a hole in her heart.

She reached for it then took it into both hands. She continued to cry aloud as she remained kneeling on the ground.

She looked at the beautiful heading on the elegant piece of stationary. On it was a hand written, black-inked note.

She wiped away tears as she tried to read Ayden's last words to her. If she had known yesterday was the last time she would see him, she would have done so much more. She would have told him how grateful she was to have him in her life and how great of a person he really was. She would have done so much more, but now she would never have that chance. She wiped away more tears, then began to read.

Dear Emma,

I am so sorry that I didn't say a proper goodbye, but I needed to get it to you somehow. Three weeks ago, the love of my life left my life. My life fell apart before my eyes. I couldn't handle it and the thought of going on without her was unbearable. Then, I got a call from the doctor telling me I had cancer and three weeks to live. I didn't know how to take it, but a thought came to me that it would be a quick way to rejoin my wife in heaven. As strange as it sounds, that night my father, who passed away years ago, gave me some advice. He told me I could either sulk the rest of my life, or I could try to make something of it. At the time, sulking sounded pretty good.

On the way home from Claire's funeral, I drove by Christmas in the Park. I saw you and immediately wanted to help. Normally I would never do such a thing, but something about you drew me in. The decision to go back and offer you dinner was the best decision I have ever made.

I never expected what came from it. Your friendship came when I needed it most. You brought to me a hope I never thought was possible, especially with the grief I felt after losing Claire. Originally, I thought I would try to listen to my father's advice and see if I could help. You may be upset but that's why when you told me about Jackson, I pushed you to visit him.

I am so glad that you agreed. To see your happiness seeing your son is a beautiful thing that really was joyous. I couldn't imagine a more beautiful sight. He really does love you.

I know you have had a difficult life, but I know it can get better. Jackson is the key to that.

When I saw that maybe I had made a difference, I began to realize it wasn't me making the difference, it was you. You showed me the true meaning of Christmas, and the true meaning of life.

Christmas is about the sacrifice Christ made for us. It is about the birth of Jesus. It is about giving. It is about hope and joy. Life is about living and doing. Life is about loving what you have and not what you could have. Life is about giving and caring. Life is about love. All of these are things I never would have realized without you. You are living proof of the meaning of Christmas and Life. You symbolize hope and love.

You have helped me to get out and do something with my life for my last days. You have helped me to see the point in life and to know what Christmas is really about. You helped me live.

So in the spirit of Christmas you have so gratefully showed me, I hope I can make one last difference with my life. My last request to you is to take back your son and live the life you both deserve.

To help with the request, I have left everything I have to you. My home, car, money and belongings. Sell it all if you would like, but my hope is that it can give you the start to a new life with Jackson.

So pick up Jackson after reading this and drive back to your new home. You have the keys. Inside will be my last gift to you. I hope you enjoy it.

So thank you, Emma. For giving me the gift of life. For giving me hope and joy. For showing me the point of life and the meaning of Christmas. For being my friend. For being you. Merry Christmas Emma.

Your friend,

Ayden

Tears welled up as Emma finished the beautiful note that Ayden had left for her. It was his last message and gift to her. She couldn't believe what he had done. He had left everything he had to her. Everything. She was still in disbelief.

She had been homeless for so long, and now, her friend had left her a house, car, and money. How could it be? She felt as though she couldn't accept any of it. How could he do that? Why? Wasn't there anyone else he could leave it to? Why her?

She tried to wrap her head around it all as she continued to cry. She read the note over and over as the tears and shock seemed to never cease. Her friend was gone and now she was left with a new life. Both hope and grief swelled inside her.

***

After hours of crying and reading the note in the hospital, she finally left. She picked up Jackson, who was given permission to go with her for the day. She would work on legally taking her son back in the next week, but for now they would just spend the day together.

Jackson had been all smiles when his birth mother had come in and told him she had a surprise for him. He too seemed to feel the spirit of Christmas. They smiled and talked as they drove toward the home Ayden had left to Emma. It was still all so surreal.

"Jackson. I was wondering if you might want to live with me?" Emma asked, trying to mask her sadness in front of her son.

"Really? A home?"

She nodded.

"Yay!" he exclaimed.

They pulled into the cul-de-sac of modern-style homes. They drove down the street till they came to a tan two-story house covered with Christmas lights and decorations.

Emma pushed the garage door opener and it began to open.

"This will be our home, Jackson," she said as she pulled the car into the garage.

"Wow," he said, trying to take it all in. He was so young, innocent, sweet and genuine. She loved him so much.

Anxiety filled her as she began to realize she was no longer homeless. It truly was bittersweet. She was giving up the life she had grown to become comfortable with for a life she knew would be great. She had all these new things, but hated the way she came upon them. Ayden had died for her to have them. She tried to push away a tear at the thought.

Nerves fluttered as she and Jackson walked toward the door into the house.

The note she had read over a hundred times said there would be one last surprise in the house. She didn't know what it would be, but she would soon find out.

She paused at the door way, looking down at her beautiful son. She smiled realizing it was Ayden who had brought them together. He had done so much for her, and now he was gone. She hoped he was reunited with the one he loved most—Claire. Emma grinned at the thought, then pushed the door open.

The sight was breathtaking. Her eyes lit up as she saw it.

"Wow!" Jackson exclaimed.

Inside were presents. There weren't just one or two. There were hundreds. Literally hundreds. They started a few feet away from the doorway and went all the way to the giant Christmas tree that she had helped him pick out. There was an entire room filled with presents, leaving no space anywhere. Wrappings of all sorts covered them. There had to be over two hundred presents. Red, green, blue, silver, and gold wrapped boxes lay all over the entire room. The sight was overwhelming.

After realizing what the room held, she slowly took a step forward. She grabbed her son's hand and they walked in together. She couldn't move much further into the room as the presents blocked the way. How could he have done this? Why? She was truly grateful. He had given her true hope and joy. She stood with Jackson, hand in hand. They stared into the room filled with endless glistening presents.

She picked up the first one in the entry; a large red wrapped box. On it was a tag. *To: Jackson. From: Santa.*

She smiled at it and handed it to Jackson. Under it she found one that said *To: Emma. From: Santa.* She laughed as she saw it. They began to unwrap their first presents in the room filled with hundreds and a giant magnificent Christmas tree in the center.

"Thank you, Ayden," she whispered aloud, grinning as tears of joy began to fall. "Merry Christmas."

Made in the USA
Middletown, DE
17 November 2016